Arkansas Concealed Handgun Carry Licensing Law

§5-73-301. Definitions.
As used in this subchapter:
(1) "Acceptable electronic format" means an electronic image produced on the person's own cellular phone or other type of portable electronic device that displays all of the information on a concealed handgun license as clearly as an original concealed handgun license;
(2) "Concealed" means to cover from observation so as to prevent public view;
(3) "Convicted" means that a person pleaded guilty or nolo contendere to or was found guilty of a criminal offense;
(4) "Handgun" means any firearm, other than a fully automatic firearm, with a barrel length of less than twelve inches (12") that is designed, made, or adapted to be fired with one (1) hand;
(5) "Licensee" means a person granted a valid license to carry a concealed handgun pursuant to this subchapter;
(6) "Parking lot" means an area, structure, or part of a structure designated for the parking of motor vehicles or a designated drop-off zone for children at a school;
(7) "Private university or private college" means an institution of higher education that is not a public university, public college, or community college as defined in § 5-73-322; and
(8) "Retired law enforcement officer" means a person who retired as a certified law enforcement officer from a local or state law enforcement agency with at least ten (10) years of experience as a law enforcement officer.
History Acts 1995, No. 411, § 1; 1995, No. 419, § 1; 1997, No. 1239, § 1; 2007, No. 664, § 1; 2007, No. 827, §§ 98, 99; 2013, No. 419, § 1; 2015, No. 1078, § 3; 2017, No. 859, § 3; 2017, No. 957, § 1.

§5-73-302. Authority to issue license.
(a) The Director of the Division of Arkansas State Police may issue a license to carry a concealed handgun to a person qualified as provided in this subchapter.
(b) (1) For new licenses issued after July 31, 2007, the license to carry a concealed handgun is valid throughout the state for a period of five (5) years from the date of issuance.
  (2) After July 31, 2007, upon renewal, an existing valid license to carry a concealed handgun shall be issued for a period of five (5) years.
(c) (1) (A) After July 31, 2007, a license or renewal of a license issued to a former elected or appointed sheriff of any county of this state shall be issued for a period of five (5) years.
   (B) The license issued to a former elected or appointed sheriff is revocable on the same grounds as other licenses.
  (2) (A) The former elected or appointed sheriff shall meet the same qualifications as all other applicants.

(B) However, the former elected or appointed sheriff is exempt from the fee prescribed by § 5-73-311(a)(2) and from the training requirements of § 5-73-309(13) for issuance.

History Acts 1995, No. 411, § 2; 1995, No. 419, § 2; 1997, No. 389, § 1; 2007, No. 1014, §§ 1, 3; 2019, No. 910, § 5736.

§5-73-303. Immunity from civil damages.

The state, a county or city, or any employee of the state, county, or city is not liable for any civil damages resulting from the issuance of a license pursuant to a provision of this subchapter.

History Acts 1995, No. 411, § 3; 1995, No. 419, § 3.

§5-73-304. Exemptions.

(a) (1) (A) A current or former certified law enforcement officer, chief of police, court bailiff, county sheriff, or retired law enforcement officer is exempt from the licensing requirements of this subchapter if otherwise authorized to carry a concealed handgun.

(B) A former certified law enforcement officer whose employment was terminated by a law enforcement agency due to disciplinary reasons or because he or she committed a disqualifying criminal offense is not exempt from the licensing requirements of this subchapter.

(2) Solely for purposes of this subchapter, an auxiliary law enforcement officer certified by the Arkansas Commission on Law Enforcement Standards and Training and approved by the county sheriff of the county where he or she is acting as an auxiliary law enforcement officer is deemed to be a certified law enforcement officer.

(b) An employee of a local detention facility is exempt from the licensing requirements of this subchapter if the employee of a local detention facility is authorized in writing as exempt from the licensing requirements of this subchapter by the chief of police or county sheriff that employs the employee of a local detention facility.

(c) The authorization prescribed in subsection (b) of this section shall be carried on the person of the employee of a local detention facility and be produced upon demand at the request of any law enforcement officer or owner or operator of any of the prohibited places as set out in § 5-73-306.

(d) A retired law enforcement officer is exempt from the licensing requirements of this subchapter if the retired law enforcement officer is permitted to carry a concealed handgun under § 12-15-202(b).

(e) As used in this section, "employee of a local detention facility" means a person who:

(1) Is employed by a county sheriff or municipality that operates a local detention facility and whose job duties include:

(A) Securing a local detention facility;

(B) Monitoring inmates in a local detention facility; and

(C) Administering the daily operation of the local detention facility; and

(2) Has completed the minimum training requirements for his or her position.

History Acts 1995, No. 411, § 2; 1995, No. 419, § 2; 1997, No. 696, § 1; 1997, No. 1239, § 8; 1999, No. 1508, §§ 1, 7; 2013, No. 415, § 1; 2013, No. 1220, § 1; 2017, No. 957, § 2.

§5-73-305. Criminal penalty.

Any person who knowingly submits a false answer to any question on an application for a license issued pursuant to this subchapter, or who knowingly submits a false document when applying for a license issued pursuant to this subchapter upon conviction is guilty of a Class B misdemeanor.
History Acts 1995, No. 411, § 2; 1995, No. 419, § 2.

§5-73-306. Prohibited places.

Except as permitted under § 5-73-322(g), a license to carry a concealed handgun issued under this subchapter does not authorize a person to carry a concealed handgun into:

(1) Any police station, sheriff's station, or Department of Arkansas State Police station;

(2) An Arkansas Highway Police Division of the Arkansas Department of Transportation facility;

(3) (A) A building of the Arkansas Department of Transportation or onto grounds adjacent to a building of the Arkansas Department of Transportation.

  (B) However, subdivision (3)(A) of this section does not apply to:

  (i) A rest area or weigh station of the Arkansas Department of Transportation; or

  (ii) A publicly owned and maintained parking lot that is a publicly accessible parking lot if the licensee is carrying a concealed handgun in his or her motor vehicle or has left the concealed handgun in his or her locked and unattended motor vehicle in the publicly owned and maintained parking lot;

(4) Any part of a detention facility, prison, jail, or residential treatment facility owned or operated by the Division of Youth Services of the Department of Human Services, including without limitation a parking lot owned, maintained, or otherwise controlled by:

  (A) The Division of Correction;

  (B) The Division of Community Correction; or

  (C) A residential treatment facility owned or operated by the Division of Youth Services of the Department of Human Services;

(5) Any courthouse, courthouse annex, or other building owned, leased, or regularly used by a county for conducting court proceedings or housing a county office unless:

  (A) The licensee is:

  (i) Employed by the county;

  (ii) A countywide elected official;

  (iii) A justice of the peace; or

  (iv) (a) Employed by a governmental entity other than the county with an office or place of employment inside the courthouse, the courthouse annex, or other building owned, leased, or regularly used by the county for conducting court proceedings or housing a county office.

(b) A licensee is limited to carrying a concealed handgun under subdivision (5)(A)(iv)(a) of this section into the courthouse, courthouse annex, or other building owned, leased, or regularly used by the county for conducting court proceedings or housing a county office where the office or place of employment of the governmental entity that employs him or her is located;

(B) The licensee's principal place of employment is within the courthouse, the courthouse annex, or other building owned, leased, or regularly used by the county for conducting court proceedings or housing a county office; and

(C) The quorum court by ordinance approves a plan that allows licensees permitted under this subdivision (5) to carry a concealed handgun into the courthouse, courthouse annex, or other building owned, leased, or regularly used by a county for conducting court proceedings as set out by the local security and emergency preparedness plan;

(6) (A) Any courtroom.

(B) However, nothing in this subchapter precludes a judge from carrying a concealed weapon or determining who will carry a concealed weapon into his or her courtroom;

(7) Any meeting place of the governing body of any governmental entity;

(8) Any meeting of the General Assembly or a committee of the General Assembly;

(9) Any state office;

(10) Any athletic event not related to firearms;

(11) (A) A portion of an establishment, except a restaurant as defined in § 3-5-1202, licensed to dispense alcoholic beverages for consumption on the premises.

(B) A person with a concealed carry endorsement under § 5-73-322(g) and who is carrying a concealed handgun may not enter an establishment under this section if the establishment either places a written notice as permitted under subdivision (18) of this section or provides notice under subdivision (19) of this section prohibiting a person with a license to possess a concealed handgun at the physical location;

(12) (A) A portion of an establishment, except a restaurant as defined in § 3-5-1202, where beer or light wine is consumed on the premises.

(B) A person with a concealed carry endorsement under § 5-73-322(g) and who is carrying a concealed handgun may not enter an establishment under this section if the establishment either places a written notice as permitted under subdivision (18) of this section or provides notice under subdivision (19) of this section prohibiting a person with a license to possess a concealed handgun at the physical location;

(13) (A) A school, college, community college, or university campus building or event.

(B) However, subdivision (13)(A) of this section does not apply to:

(i) A kindergarten through grade twelve (K-12) private school operated by a church or other place of worship that:

(a) Is located on the developed property of the kindergarten through grade twelve (K-12) private school;

(b) Allows the licensee to carry a concealed handgun into the church or other place of worship under this section; and

(c) Allows the licensee to possess a concealed handgun on the developed property of the kindergarten through grade twelve (K-12) private school under § 5-73-119(e);

(ii) A kindergarten through grade twelve (K-12) private school or a prekindergarten private school that through its governing board or director has set forth the rules and circumstances under which the licensee may carry a concealed handgun into a building or event of the kindergarten through grade twelve (K-12) private school or the prekindergarten private school;

(iii) Participation in an authorized firearms-related activity;

(iv) Carrying a concealed handgun as authorized under § 5-73-322; or

(v) A publicly owned and maintained parking lot of a college, community college, or university if the licensee is carrying a concealed handgun in his or her motor vehicle or has left the concealed handgun in his or her locked and unattended motor vehicle;

(14) Inside the passenger terminal of any airport, except that no person is prohibited from carrying any legal firearm into the passenger terminal if the firearm is encased for shipment for purposes of checking the firearm as baggage to be lawfully transported on any aircraft;

(15) (A) Any church or other place of worship.

(B) However, this subchapter does not preclude a church or other place of worship from determining who may carry a concealed handgun into the church or other place of worship.

(C) A person with a concealed carry endorsement under § 5-73-322(g) and who is carrying a concealed handgun may not enter a church or other place of worship under this section if the church or other place of worship either places a written notice as permitted under subdivision (18) of this section or provides notice under subdivision (19) of this section prohibiting a person with a license to possess a concealed handgun at the physical location;

(16) Any place where the carrying of a firearm is prohibited by federal law;

(17) Any place where a parade or demonstration requiring a permit is being held, and the licensee is a participant in the parade or demonstration;

(18) (A) (i) Any place at the discretion of the person or entity exercising control over the physical location of the place by placing at each entrance to the place a written notice clearly readable at a distance of not less than ten feet (10') that "carrying a handgun is prohibited".

(ii) (a) If the place does not have a roadway entrance, there shall be a written notice placed anywhere upon the premises of the place.

(b) In addition to the requirement of subdivision (18)(A)(ii)(a) of this section, there shall be at least one (1) written notice posted within every three (3) acres of a place with no roadway entrance.

(iii) A written notice as described in subdivision (18)(A)(i) of this section is not required for a private home.

(iv) Any licensee entering a private home shall notify the occupant that the licensee is carrying a concealed handgun.

(B) Subdivision (18)(A) of this section does not apply if the place is:

(i) A public university, public college, or community college, as defined in § 5-73-322, and the licensee is carrying a concealed handgun as provided under § 5-73-322;

(ii) A publicly owned and maintained parking lot if the licensee is carrying a concealed handgun in his or her motor vehicle or has left the concealed handgun in his or her locked and unattended motor vehicle; or

(iii) A parking lot of a private employer and the licensee is carrying a concealed handgun as provided under § 5-73-326.

(C) The person or entity exercising control over the physical location of a place that does not use his, her, or its authority under this subdivision (18) to prohibit a person from possessing a concealed handgun is immune from a claim for monetary damages arising from or related to the decision not to place at each entrance to the place a written notice under this subdivision (18);

(19) (A) (i) A place owned or operated by a private entity that prohibits the carrying of a concealed handgun that posts a written notice as described under subdivision (18)(A) of this section.

(ii) (a) A place owned or operated by a private entity that chooses not to post a written notice as described under subdivision (18)(A) of this section may provide written or verbal notification to a licensee who is carrying a concealed handgun at the place owned or operated by a private entity that carrying of a concealed handgun is prohibited.

(b) A licensee who receives written or verbal notification under subdivision (19)(A)(ii)(a) of this section is deemed to have violated this subdivision (19) if the licensee while carrying a concealed handgun either remains at or returns to the place owned or operated by the private entity.

(B) A place owned or operated by a private entity under this subdivision (19) includes without limitation:

(i) A private university or private college;

(ii) A church or other place of worship;

(iii) An establishment, except a restaurant as defined in § 3-5-1202, licensed to dispense alcoholic beverages for consumption on the premises; and

(iv) An establishment, except a restaurant as defined in § 3-5-1202, where beer or light wine is consumed on the premises; or

(20) A posted firearm-sensitive area, as approved by the Department of Arkansas State Police under § 5-73-325, located at:

(A) The Arkansas State Hospital;

(B) The University of Arkansas for Medical Sciences; or

(C) A collegiate athletic event.

History Acts 1995, No. 411, § 2; 1995, No. 419, § 2; 1997, No. 1239, § 2; 2003, No. 1110, § 1; 2007, No. 664, § 2; 2009, No. 294, § 28; 2011, No. 758, § 1; 2013, No. 67, § 1; 2013, No. 226, §§ 3, 4; 2013, No. 1390, § 2; 2015, No. 933, § 2; 2015, No. 1078, §§ 4-7; 2015, No. 1175, § 1; 2015, No. 1259, § 2; 2017, No. 562, §§ 2-5; 2017, No. 707, § 5; 2017, No. 859, §§ 4-6; 2017, No. 1071, § 2; 2017, No. 1090, § 1; 2019, No. 910, § 683; 2019, No. 431, § 2.

§5-73-307. List of license holders.

(a) The Department of Arkansas State Police shall maintain an automated listing of license holders, and this information shall be available online, upon request, at any time, to any law enforcement agency through the Arkansas Crime Information Center.

(b) Nothing in this subchapter shall be construed to require or allow the registration, documentation, or providing of a serial number with regard to any firearm.

History Acts 1995, No. 411, § 2; 1995, No. 419, § 2; 1997, No. 1239, § 3; 2007, No. 827, § 100.

§5-73-308. License -- Issuance or denial.

(a) (1) (A) The Director of the Division of Arkansas State Police may deny a license if within the preceding five (5) years the applicant has been found guilty of one (1) or more crimes of violence constituting a misdemeanor or for the offense of carrying a weapon.

(B) The director may revoke a license if the licensee has been found guilty of one (1) or more crimes of violence within the preceding three (3) years.

(2) Subdivision (a)(1) of this section does not apply to a misdemeanor that has been expunged or for which the imposition of sentence was suspended.

(3) Upon notification by any law enforcement agency or a court and subsequent written verification, the director shall suspend a license or the processing of an application for a license if the licensee or applicant is arrested or formally charged with a crime that would disqualify the licensee or applicant from having a license under this subchapter until final disposition of the case.

(b) (1) The director may deny a license to carry a concealed handgun if the county sheriff or chief of police, if applicable, of the applicant's place of residence or the director or the director's designee submits an affidavit that the applicant has been or is reasonably likely to be a danger to himself or herself or others or to the community at large, as demonstrated by past patterns of behavior or participation in an incident involving unlawful violence or threats of unlawful violence, or if the applicant is under a criminal investigation at the time of applying for a license to carry a concealed handgun.

(2) Within one hundred twenty (120) days after the date of receipt of the items listed in § 5-73-311(a), the director shall:

(A) Issue the license; or

(B) Deny the application based solely on the ground that the applicant fails to qualify under the criteria listed in this subchapter.

(3)(A) If the director denies the application, the director shall notify the applicant in writing, stating the grounds for denial.

(B) The decision of the director is subject to appeal under the Arkansas Administrative Procedure Act, § 25-15-201 et seq.

History Acts 1995, No. 411, § 2; 1995, No. 419, § 2; 1997, No. 1239, § 4; 2011, No. 758, § 2; 2013, No. 1328, § 1; 2019, No. 910, § 5737.

§5-73-309. License -- Requirements.

The Director of the Division of Arkansas State Police shall issue a license to carry a concealed handgun if the applicant:

(1) Is a citizen of the United States or a permanent legal resident;

(2) (A) Is a resident of the state and has been a resident continuously for ninety (90) days or longer immediately preceding the filing of the application.

(B) However, subdivision (2)(A) of this section does not apply to any:

(i) Active duty member of the United States Armed Forces who submits documentation of his or her active duty status; or

(ii) Spouse of an active duty member of the United States Armed Forces who submits documentation of his or her spouse's active duty status;

(3) Is at least:

(A) Twenty-one (21) years of age; or

(B) Eighteen (18) years of age and is:

(i) Currently a federally recognized commissioned or noncommissioned officer or an enlisted member on active duty in the United States Armed Forces;

(ii) In the National Guard or a reserve component of the United States Armed Forces; or

(iii) A former member of the United States Armed Forces who has been honorably discharged;

(4) Does not suffer from a mental or physical infirmity that prevents the safe handling of a handgun and has not threatened or attempted suicide;

(5) Has not been convicted of a felony in a court of this state, of any other state, or of the United States unless:

(A) The applicant is subsequently granted a pardon by the Governor or the President of the United States explicitly restoring his or her ability to possess a firearm;

(B) The applicant was sentenced prior to March 13, 1995, and the record of conviction has been sealed or expunged under Arkansas law; or

(C) The applicant's offense was dismissed and sealed or expunged under § 16-93-301 et seq. or § 16-98-303(g).

(6) Is not subject to any federal, state, or local law that makes it unlawful to receive, possess, or transport any firearm, and has had his or her background check successfully completed through the Division of Arkansas State Police and the Federal Bureau of Investigation's National Instant Criminal Background Check System;

(7) (A) Does not chronically or habitually abuse a controlled substance to the extent that his or her normal faculties are impaired.

(B) It is presumed that an applicant chronically and habitually uses a controlled substance to the extent that his or her faculties are impaired if the applicant has been voluntarily or involuntarily committed to a treatment facility for the abuse of a controlled substance or has been found guilty of a crime under the provisions of the Uniform Controlled Substances Act, § 5-64-101 et seq., or a similar law of any other state or the United States relating to a controlled substance within the three-year period immediately preceding the date on which the application is submitted;

(8) (A) Does not chronically or habitually use an alcoholic beverage to the extent that his or her normal faculties are impaired.

(B) It is presumed that an applicant chronically and habitually uses an alcoholic beverage to the extent that his or her normal faculties are impaired if the applicant has been voluntarily or involuntarily committed as an alcoholic to a treatment facility or has been convicted of two (2) or more offenses related to the use of alcohol under a law of this state or similar law of any other state or the United States within the three-year period immediately preceding the date on which the application is submitted;

(9) Desires a legal means to carry a concealed handgun to defend himself or herself;

(10) Has not been adjudicated mentally incompetent;

(11) (A) Has not been voluntarily or involuntarily committed to a mental institution or mental health treatment facility.

(B) An applicant who is a veteran who voluntarily sought mental health treatment at a mental health institution or mental health treatment facility may obtain a license under this subchapter if a circuit court grants his or her petition under § 5-73-327;

(12) Is not a fugitive from justice or does not have an active warrant for his or her arrest;

(13) Has satisfactorily completed a training course as prescribed and approved by the director; and

(14) Signs a statement of allegiance to the United States Constitution and the Arkansas Constitution.

History Acts 1995, No. 411, § 2; 1995, No. 419, § 2; 1997, No. 368, § 1; 1997, No. 1239, § 10; 1999, No. 51, § 1; 2003, No. 545, §§ 1, 5; 2007, No. 198, § 1; 2007, No. 664, § 3; 2013, No. 989, § 1; 2015, No. 105, § 1; 2015, No. 649, § 1; 2019, No. 910, §§ 5738, 5739; 2019, No. 917, § 1; 2019, No. 1038, § 1.

5-73-310. Application form.

The application for a license to carry a concealed handgun shall be completed, under oath, on a form promulgated by the Director of the Division of Arkansas State Police and shall include only:

(1) The name, address, place and date of birth, race, and sex of the applicant;

(2) The driver's license number or Social Security number of the applicant;

(3) Any previous address of the applicant for the two (2) years preceding the date of the application;

(4) A statement that the applicant is in compliance with criteria contained within §§ 5-73-308(a) and 5-73-309;

(5) A statement that the applicant has been furnished a copy of this subchapter and is acquainted with the truth and understanding of this subchapter;

(6) A conspicuous warning that the application is executed under oath, and that a knowingly false answer to any question or the knowing submission of any false document by the applicant subjects the applicant to:

(A) Criminal prosecution and precludes any future license's being issued to the applicant; and

(B) Immediate revocation if the license has already been issued;

(7) A statement that the applicant desires a legal means to carry a concealed handgun to defend himself or herself;

(8) (A) A statement of whether the applicant is applying for:

(i) An unrestricted license, that allows the person to carry any handgun; or

(ii) A restricted license, that allows the person to carry any handgun other than a semiautomatic handgun.

(B) (i) An applicant requesting an unrestricted license shall establish proficiency in the use of a semiautomatic handgun.

(ii) An applicant requesting a restricted license shall establish proficiency in the use of a handgun and may use any kind of handgun when establishing proficiency; and

(9) A statement of whether or not the applicant has been found guilty of a crime of violence or domestic abuse.

History Acts 1995, No. 411, § 2; 1995, No. 419, § 2; 1997, No. 1239, § 5; 1999, No. 786, § 1; 2019, No. 910, § 5740.

§5-73-311. Application procedure.

(a) The applicant for a license to carry a concealed handgun shall submit the following to the Division of Arkansas State Police:

(1) A completed application, as described in § 5-73-310;

(2) A nonrefundable license fee of fifty dollars ($50.00), except that the nonrefundable license fee is twenty-five dollars ($25.00) if the applicant is sixty-five (65) years of age or older;

(3)(A) A full set of fingerprints of the applicant.

(B) In the event a legible set of fingerprints, as determined by the division and the Federal Bureau of Investigation, cannot be obtained after a minimum of two (2) attempts, the Director of the Division of Arkansas State Police shall determine eligibility in accordance with criteria that the division shall establish by promulgating rules.

(C) Costs for processing the set of fingerprints as required in subdivision (a)(3)(A) of this section shall be borne by the applicant;

(4) (A) A waiver authorizing the division access to any medical, criminal, or other records concerning the applicant and permitting access to all of the applicant's criminal records.

(B) If a check of the applicant's criminal records uncovers any unresolved felony arrests over ten (10) years old, then the applicant shall obtain a letter of reference from the county sheriff, prosecuting attorney, or circuit judge of the county where the applicant resides that states that to the best of the county sheriff's, prosecuting attorney's, or circuit judge's knowledge that the applicant is of good character and free of any felony convictions.

(C) The division shall maintain the confidentiality of the medical, criminal, or other records; and

(5) A digital photograph of the applicant or a release authorization to obtain a digital photograph of the applicant from another source.

(b) (1) Upon receipt of the items listed in subsection (a) of this section, the department shall forward the full set of fingerprints of the applicant to the appropriate agencies for state and federal processing.

(2) (A) The division shall forward a notice of the applicant's application to the sheriff of the applicant's county of residence and, if applicable, the police chief of the applicant's municipality of residence.

(B) (i) The sheriff of the applicant's county of residence and, if applicable, the police chief of the applicant's municipality of residence may participate, at his or her discretion, in the process by submitting a voluntary report to the division containing any readily discoverable information that he or she feels may be pertinent to the licensing of any applicant.

(ii) The reporting under subdivision (b)(2)(B)(i) of this section shall be made within thirty (30) days after the date the notice of the application was sent by the division.

(c) A concealed handgun license issued, renewed, or obtained under § 5-73-314 or § 5-73-319 after December 31, 2007, shall bear a digital photograph of the licensee.

History Acts 1995, No. 411, § 2; 1995, No. 419, § 2; 1997, No. 1239, § 9; 1997, No. 1251, § 1; 1999, No. 487, § 1; 2007, No. 664, § 4; 2009, No. 748, § 42; 2013, No. 1271, § 1; 2019, No. 910, §§ 5741 to 5745; 2019, No. 61, § 1; 2019, No. 188, § 1.

§5-73-312. Revocation.

(a) (1) A license to carry a concealed handgun issued under this subchapter shall be revoked if the licensee becomes ineligible under the criteria set forth in § 5-73-308(a) or § 5-73-309.

(2) (A) Any law enforcement officer making an arrest of a licensee for a violation of this subchapter or any other statutory violation that requires revocation of a license to carry a concealed handgun shall confiscate the license and forward it to the Director of the Division of Arkansas State Police.

(B) The license shall be held until a determination of the charge is finalized, with the appropriate disposition of the license after the determination.

(b) When the Division of Arkansas State Police receives notification from any law enforcement agency or court that a licensee has been found guilty or has pleaded guilty or nolo contendere to any crime involving the use of a weapon, the license issued under this subchapter is immediately revoked.

(c) The director shall revoke the license of any licensee who has pleaded guilty or nolo contendere to or been found guilty of an alcohol-related offense committed while carrying a handgun.

History Acts 1995, No. 411, §§ 2, 4, 5; 1995, No. 419, §§ 2, 4, 5; 1997, No. 1239, § 11; 2003, No. 545, § 4; 2007, No. 827, § 101; 2019, No. 910, §§ 5746, 5747.

§5-73-313. Expiration and renewal.

(a) Except as provided in subdivision (f)(1) of this section, the licensee may renew his or her license no more than ninety (90) days prior to the expiration date by submitting to the Department of Arkansas State Police:

(1) A renewal form prescribed by the department;

(2) A verified statement that the licensee remains qualified pursuant to the criteria specified in §§ 5-73-308(a) and 5-73-309;

(3) A renewal fee of twenty-five dollars ($25.00);

(4) A certification or training form properly completed by the licensee's training instructor reflecting that the licensee's training was conducted; and

(5) A digital photograph of the licensee or a release authorization to obtain a digital photograph of the licensee from another source.

(b) The license shall be renewed upon receipt of the completed renewal application, a digital photograph of the licensee, and appropriate payment of fees subject to a background investigation conducted pursuant to this subchapter that did not reveal any disqualifying offense or unresolved arrest that would disqualify a licensee under this subchapter.

(c) Additionally, a licensee who fails to file a renewal application on or before the expiration date shall renew his or her license by paying a late fee of fifteen dollars ($15.00).

(d) (1) No license shall be renewed six (6) months or more after its expiration date, and the license is deemed to be permanently expired.

(2) (A) A person whose license has been permanently expired may reapply for licensure.

(B) An application for licensure and fees pursuant to §§ 5-73-308(a), 5-73-309, and 5-73-311(a) shall be submitted, and a new background investigation shall be conducted.

(e) A new criminal background investigation shall be conducted when an applicant applies for renewal of a license. Costs for processing a new background check shall be paid by the applicant.

(f) (1) An active duty member of the United States Armed Forces, a member of the National Guard, or a member of a reserve component of the United States Armed Forces, who is on active duty outside this state may renew his or her license within thirty (30) days after the person returns to this state by submitting to the department:

(A) Proof of assignment outside of this state on the expiration date of the license; and

(B) The items listed in subdivisions (a)(1)-(5) of this section.

(2) Subsections (c) and (d) of this section shall not apply to a person who renews his or her license under subdivision (f)(1) of this section.

History Acts 1995, No. 411, § 2; 1995, No. 419, § 2; 1997, No. 1239, §§ 6, 12; 1999, No. 487, § 2; 2003, No. 545, § 2; 2005, No. 881, § 1; 2007, No. 664, § 5; 2019, No. 61, § 2; 2019, No. 188, § 2.

§5-73-314. Lost, destroyed, or duplicate license -- Change of address.

(a) Within thirty (30) days after the changing of a permanent address, or within thirty (30) days after having a license to carry a concealed handgun lost, the licensee shall notify the Director of the Division of Arkansas State Police in writing of the change or loss.

(b) If a license to carry a concealed handgun is lost or destroyed, or a duplicate is requested, the person to whom the license to carry a concealed handgun was issued shall comply with the provisions of subsection (a) of this section and may obtain a duplicate license or replacement license upon:

(1) Paying the Division of Arkansas State Police a fee established by the director under the Arkansas Administrative Procedure Act, § 25-15-201 et seq.; and

(2) Furnishing a notarized statement to the division that the license to carry a concealed handgun has been lost or destroyed or that a duplicate is requested.

(c) The fee described in subdivision (b)(1) of this section shall be reduced by fifty percent (50%) if a person sixty-five (65) years of age or older is requesting a replacement or duplicate license under this section.

History Acts 1995, No. 411, § 2; 1995, No. 419, § 2; 2011, No. 758, § 3; 2013, No. 1271, § 2; 2015, No. 1155, § 15' 2019, No. 910, §§ 5748, 5749.

§5-73-315. Authority to carry concealed handgun -- Identification of licensee.

(a) Any licensee possessing a valid license issued pursuant to this subchapter may carry a concealed handgun.

(b) The licensee shall:

(1) Carry the license, or an electronic copy of the license in an acceptable electronic format, together with valid identification, at any time when the licensee is carrying a concealed handgun; and

(2) Display both the license, or an electronic copy of the license in an acceptable electronic format, and proper identification upon demand by a law enforcement officer.

(c) The presentment of proof of a license to carry a concealed handgun in electronic form does not:

(1) Authorize a search of any other content of an electronic device without a search warrant or probable cause; or

(2) Expand or restrict the authority of a law enforcement officer to conduct a search or investigation.

History Acts 1995, No. 411, § 2; 1995, No. 419, § 2; 2007, No. 827, § 102; 2013, No. 419, § 2.

§5-73-316. Fees.

Any fee collected by the Department of Arkansas State Police pursuant to this subchapter shall be deposited into the Department of Arkansas State Police Fund.

History Acts 1995, No. 411, § 2; 1995, No. 419, § 2.

§5-73-317. Rules.

The Director of the Division of Arkansas State Police may promulgate rules to permit the efficient administration of this subchapter.

History Acts 1995, No. 411, § 8; 1995, No. 419, § 8; 2019, No. 910, § 5750; 2019, No. 315, § 172

§5-73-318. Instructor review of applications.

(a) An instructor authorized to conduct a training course required by this subchapter shall check the application of a student for completeness, accuracy, and legibility.

(b) An instructor who repeatedly fails to comply with subsection (a) of this section may have his or her license to conduct a training course revoked.

History Acts 1997, No. 1239, § 7.

§5-73-319. Transfer of a license to Arkansas.

(a) Any person who becomes a resident of Arkansas who has a valid license to carry a concealed handgun issued by a reciprocal state may apply to transfer his or her license to Arkansas by submitting the following to the Department of Arkansas State Police:

(1) The person's current reciprocal state license;

(2) Two (2) properly completed fingerprint cards;

(3) A nonrefundable license fee of thirty-five dollars ($35.00);

(4) Any fee charged by a state or federal agency for a criminal history check; and

(5) A digital photograph of the person or a release authorization to obtain a digital photograph of the person from another source.

(b) After July 31, 2007, the newly transferred license is valid for a period of five (5) years from the date of issuance and binds the holder to all Arkansas laws and rules regarding the carrying of the concealed handgun.

History Acts 2003, No. 545, § 3; 2007, No. 664, § 26; 2007, No. 1014, § 2, 2019, No. 315, § 173.

§5-73-320. License for certain members of the Arkansas National Guard or a reserve component or active duty military personnel.

(a) The Division of Arkansas State Police may issue a license under this subchapter to a person who:

(1) Is currently serving as an active duty member of, or has recently been honorably discharged from, the United States Armed Forces, the National Guard, or a reserve component of the United States Armed Forces;

(2) Submits the following documents:

(A) A completed concealed handgun license application as prescribed by the division;

(B) A form specified by the Director of the Division of Arkansas State Police reflecting the fingerprints of the applicant;

(C) A properly completed and dated certificate from a concealed handgun carry training instructor who is registered with the division;

(D) A letter dated and personally signed by a commanding officer or his or her designee stating that the applicant is of good character and sound judgment;

(E) A form, as designated by the division, showing that the applicant has met the military qualification requirements for issuance and operation of a handgun within one (1) year of the application date;

(F) A copy of the face or photograph side of a current uniformed services of the United States identification card, if the applicant is a member of the United States Armed Forces; and

(G) An electronic passport-style photo of the applicant, if the applicant does not hold an Arkansas driver's license or identification card; and

(3) Submits any required fees.

(b) Except as otherwise specifically stated in this section, the license issued under this section is subject to the provisions of this subchapter and any rules promulgated under § 5-73-317.

History Acts 2005, No. 1868, § 1; 2007, No. 664, § 7; 2007, No. 1014, § 3; 2013, No. 989, § 2; 2017, No. 1017, § 1; 2019, No. 910, § 5751.

§5-73-321. Recognition of other states' licenses.

A person in possession of a valid license to carry a concealed handgun issued to the person by another state is entitled to the privileges and subject to the restrictions prescribed by this subchapter.

History Acts 2009, No. 748, § 43; 2013, No. 1089, § 1.

§5-73-322. Concealed handguns in a university, college, or community college building.

(a) (1) As used in this section, "public university, public college, or community college" means an institution that:

   (A) Regularly receives budgetary support from the state government;

   (B) Is part of the University of Arkansas or Arkansas State University systems; or

   (C) Is required to report to the Arkansas Higher Education Coordinating Board.

   (2) "Public university, public college, or community college" includes without limitation a public technical institute.

   (3) "Public university, public college, or community college" does not include a private university or private college solely because:

   (A) Students attending the private university or private college receive state-supported scholarships; or

   (B) The private university or private college voluntarily reports to the Arkansas Higher Education Coordinating Board.

(b) A licensee who has completed the training required under subsection (g) of this section may possess a concealed handgun in the buildings and on the grounds of a public university, public college, or community college, whether owned or leased by the public university, public college, or community college, unless otherwise prohibited by this section or § 5-73-306.

(c) (1) A licensee may possess a concealed handgun in the buildings and on the grounds of a private university or private college unless otherwise prohibited by this section or § 5-73-306 if the private university or private college does not adopt a policy expressly disallowing the carrying of a concealed handgun in the buildings and on the grounds of the private university or private college.

   (2) (A) A private university or private college that adopts a policy expressly disallowing the carrying of a concealed handgun in the buildings and on the grounds of the private university or private college shall post notices as described in § 5-73-306(18).

   (B) A private university or private college that adopts a policy only allowing carrying of a concealed handgun under this section shall post notices as described in § 5-73-306(18) and subdivision (c)(2)(C) of this section.

   (C) If a private university or private college permits carrying a concealed handgun under this section, the private university or private college may revise any sign or notice required to be posted under § 5-73-306(18) to indicate that carrying a concealed handgun under this section is permitted.

(d) The storage of a handgun in a university or college-operated student dormitory or residence hall is prohibited under § 5-73-119(c).

(e) (1) A licensee who may carry a concealed handgun in the buildings and on the grounds of a public university, public college, or community college under this section may not carry a concealed handgun into a location in which an official meeting lasting no more than nine (9) hours is being conducted in accordance with documented grievance and disciplinary procedures as established by the public university, public college, or community college if:

(A) At least twenty-four (24) hours' notice is given to participants of the official meeting;

(B) Notice is posted on the door of or each entryway into the location in which the official meeting is being conducted that possession of a concealed handgun by a licensee under this section is prohibited during the official meeting; and

(C) The area of a building prohibited under this subdivision (e)(1) is no larger than necessary to complete the grievance or disciplinary meeting.

(2) A person who knowingly violates subdivision (e)(1) of this section upon conviction is guilty of:

(A) A violation for a first offense and subject to a fine not exceeding one hundred dollars ($100); and

(B) A Class C misdemeanor for a second or subsequent offense.

(f) This section does not affect a licensee's ability to store a concealed handgun in his or her vehicle under § 5-73-306(13)(B)(v).

(g) (1) A licensee who intends to carry a concealed handgun in the buildings and on the grounds of a public university, public college, or community college is required to complete a training course approved by the Director of the Division of Arkansas State Police.

(2) (A) Training required under this subsection shall:

(i) Not be required to be renewed;

(ii) Consist of a course of up to eight (8) hours;

(iii) Be offered at the training instructor's option at concealed carry training courses; and

(iv) Cost no more than a nominal amount.

(B) The director may waive up to four (4) hours of the training required under this subsection for a licensee based on the licensee's prior training attended within ten (10) years of applying for the endorsement provided for under subdivision (g)(3) of this section on appropriate topics.

(3) A licensee who completes a training course under this subsection shall be given a concealed carry endorsement by the Division of Arkansas State Police on his or her license to carry a concealed handgun indicating that the person is permitted to possess and carry a concealed handgun in the buildings and on the grounds of a public university, public college, or community college.

(h) A licensee who completes a training course and obtains a concealed carry endorsement under subsection (g) of this section is exempted from the prohibitions and restrictions on:

(1) Carrying a firearm in a publicly owned building or facility under § 5-73-122, if the firearm is a concealed handgun; and

(2) Carrying a concealed handgun in a prohibited place listed under § 5-73-306(7)-(12), (14), (15), and (17), unless otherwise prohibited under § 5-73-306(19) or § 5-73-306(20).

(i) The division shall maintain a list of licensees who have successfully completed a training course under subsection (g) of this section.

(j) (1) Unless possession of a concealed handgun is a requirement of a licensee's job description, the possession of a concealed handgun under this section is a personal choice made by the licensee and not a requirement of the employing public university, public college, or community college.

(2) A licensee who possesses a concealed handgun in the buildings and on the grounds of a public university, public college, or community college at which the licensee is employed is not:

(A) Acting in the course of or scope of his or her employment when possessing or using a concealed handgun;

(B) Entitled to worker's compensation benefits for injuries arising from his or her own negligent acts in possessing or using a concealed handgun;

(C) Immune from personal liability with respect to possession or use of a concealed handgun; or

(D) Permitted to carry a concealed handgun openly or in any other manner in which the concealed handgun is visible to ordinary observation.

(3) A public university, public college, or community college is immune from a claim for monetary damages arising from or related to a licensee's use of, or failure to use, a concealed handgun if the licensee elects to possess a concealed handgun under this section.

History Acts 2013, No. 226, § 5; 2015, No. 1155, § 16; 2017, No. 562, § 6; 2017, No. 859, §§ 7, 8; 2019, No. 910, §§ 5752 to 5755.

§5-73-323. Parole board exemptions.

A member of the Parole Board, a board investigator, or a parole revocation judge who has been issued a license to carry a concealed handgun by the Department of Arkansas State Police under this subchapter may carry his or her concealed handgun into a building in which or a location on which a law enforcement officer may carry a handgun if the board member, board investigator, or parole revocation judge is on official business of the board.

History Acts 2013, No. 320, § 2.

§5-73-324. Firearm rights shall not be infringed.

(a) A license to carry a concealed handgun issued under this subchapter shall not be denied, suspended, or revoked because a person was lawfully exercising his or her rights to carry a firearm under the United States Constitution, Amendment 2, the Arkansas Constitution, Article 2, § 5, or the Arkansas Code.

(b) The Department of Arkansas State Police shall not promulgate any rule and shall amend any existing rule that would result in a licensee having his or her license to carry a concealed handgun suspended or revoked solely because he or she possessed a handgun and the possession was not in violation of any criminal offense or § 5-73-306.

History Acts 2017, No. 486, § 1.

§5-73-325. Firearm-sensitive areas -- Security plan approval.

(a) (1) The following entities may submit a security plan to the Department of Arkansas State Police for approval that designates certain areas as a firearm-sensitive area where possession of a concealed handgun by a licensee under this subchapter is prohibited:

(A) The Arkansas State Hospital;

(B) The University of Arkansas for Medical Sciences; and

(C) (i) An institution of higher education that hosts or sponsors a collegiate athletic event.

(ii) A firearm-sensitive area under subdivision (a)(1)(C)(i) of this section is limited to an area where a collegiate athletic event is held.

(2) A security plan submitted under this section shall include the following information and corresponding security measures:

(A) Total projected attendance;

(B) Number of entrances and exits;

(C) Number of on-site private security personnel;

(D) Number of on-site law enforcement officers;

(E) Number of on-site first responders;

(F) Location of parking areas and number of motor vehicles projected to use the parking areas;

(G) Routes for emergency vehicles;

(H) Locations of all restrooms, stairs, and elevators;

(I) Evacuation procedures;

(J) Security communication protocol;

(K) Location of emergency vehicles;

(L) Public communication protocol; and

(M) Bomb threat and active shooter procedures.

(b) Security measures under this section shall include without limitation:

(1) Security personnel or law enforcement officers on-site;

(2) Use of a magnetometer or other metal-detecting device designed to detect a weapon;

(3) Barricades; or

(4) Other measures or devices designed to protect the public from a security threat.

(c) (1) An entity shall submit a security plan to the department under this section annually or no later than five (5) days before a scheduled collegiate athletic event.

(2) The department shall approve or disapprove a security plan for a scheduled collegiate athletic event within seventy-two (72) hours of the receipt of the security plan.

(3) Otherwise the department shall approve or disapprove a security plan within ten (10) business days.

(d) Upon approval of a security plan, an entity shall post a notification at all firearm-sensitive areas that possession of a concealed handgun is prohibited.

(e) A security plan submitted under this section is exempt from public disclosure under the Freedom of Information Act of 1967, § 25-19-101 et seq.

History Acts 2017, No. 859, § 9.

§5-73-326. Licensee rights -- Private employer parking lot.

(a) A private employer shall not prohibit an employee who is a licensee from transporting or storing a legally owned handgun in the employee's private motor vehicle in the private employer's parking lot when:

 (1) The handgun:

  (A) Is lawfully possessed;

  (B) Is stored out of sight inside a locked private motor vehicle in the private employer's parking lot; and

  (C) (i) Is stored inside a locked personal handgun storage container that is designed for the safe storage of a handgun.

   (ii) An employee is not required to store the handgun in the personal handgun storage container as required in subdivision (a)(1)(C)(i) of this section until he or she is exiting his or her private motor vehicle; and

 (2) The employee has in his or her possession the key to the personal handgun storage container as required by subdivision (a)(1)(C)(i) of this section.

(b) A private employer shall not prohibit or attempt to prevent an employee who is a licensee from entering the parking lot of the private employer's place of business because the employee's private motor vehicle contains a handgun if:

 (1) The handgun is kept for lawful purposes;

 (2) The handgun is concealed within the employee's private motor vehicle; and

 (3) The employee stores the handgun in his or her motor vehicle in accordance with subdivisions (a)(1)(A)-(C) of this section.

(c) An employer has the right to:

 (1) Prohibit a person who is not an employee from storing a handgun in the employee's motor vehicle in the private employer's parking lot; and

 (2) Prohibit a licensee's entry onto the private employer's place of business or parking lot because the person's private motor vehicle contains a handgun in the following circumstances:

  (A) The parking lot is a prohibited place specifically listed in § 5-73-306;

  (B) The parking lot is on the grounds of an owner-occupied single-family detached residence or a tenant-occupied single-family detached residence and the single-family detached residence or tenant-occupied single-family detached residence is being used as a residence;

  (C) The private employer reasonably believes that the employee is in illegal possession of the handgun;

  (D) The employee is operating a private employer-owned motor vehicle during and in the course of the employee's duties on behalf of the private employer, except when the employee is required to transport or store a firearm as part of the employee's duties;

  (E) The private motor vehicle is not permitted in the parking lot for reasons unrelated to the employee's transportation, storage, or possession of a handgun;

  (F) The employee is the subject of an active or pending employment disciplinary proceeding; or

(G) The employee, at any time after being issued a license to carry a concealed handgun, has been adjudicated mentally incompetent or not guilty in a legal proceeding by reason of mental disease or defect.

(d) This section does not prevent a private employer from prohibiting a person who is not licensed or who fails to transport or store the handgun in accordance with subdivisions (a)(1)(A)-(C) of this section from transporting or storing a handgun in the parking lot or from entering onto the private employer's place of business or the private employer's parking lot.

(e) A former employee who possesses a handgun in his or her private motor vehicle under this section is not criminally liable for possessing the handgun in his or her private motor vehicle in his or her former private employer's parking lot while the former employee is physically leaving the private employer's parking lot immediately following his or her termination or other reason for ceasing employment with the former private employer.

History Acts 2017, No. 1071, § 3.

§5-73-327. Discharged veterans.

(a) As used in this section:

(1) "Mental health institution or mental health treatment facility" means a public or private facility where a person may voluntarily admit himself or herself for mental health treatment; and

(2) "Veteran" means a person who:

(A) Served on active duty in the United States Armed Forces for a period of more than one hundred eighty (180) days and was discharged or released from active duty with other than a dishonorable discharge;

(B) Was discharged or released from active duty in the United States Armed Forces because of a service-connected disability; or

(C) As a member of a reserve component of the United States Armed Forces under an order to active duty, not to include training, was discharged or released from duty with other than a dishonorable discharge.

(b) (1) A veteran who voluntarily seeks and completes mental health treatment in a mental health institution or mental health treatment facility may obtain a license to carry a concealed handgun under this subchapter by filing a petition in the circuit court where the veteran resides.

(2) However, the veteran may not obtain a license to carry a concealed handgun under this subchapter until at least two (2) years after he or she completed mental health treatment in a mental health institution or mental health treatment facility.

(c) (1) A petition under this section shall request a judicial determination that the petitioner is mentally fit and that his or her past voluntary commitment to a mental institution or mental health treatment facility would currently not have a negative impact on the petitioner's ability to responsibly possess a license to carry a concealed handgun.

(2) A petitioner shall also provide the circuit court with a limited medical waiver that would allow the circuit court and the prosecuting attorney access

to and the ability to request any medical record that concerns the petitioner's mental health treatment at issue.

(d) (1) A copy of a petition under this section shall be served on the prosecuting attorney within thirty (30) days of the filing of the petition.

(2) The prosecuting attorney may appear, support, object to, or present evidence relevant to the petition.

(e) The circuit court shall consider evidence in an open proceeding, including evidence offered by the petitioner concerning:

(1) The circumstances that led to the petitioner voluntarily seeking mental health treatment;

(2) The petitioner's certified mental health records;

(3) The petitioner's certified criminal history;

(4) The petitioner's reputation; and

(5) Changes in the petitioner's condition or circumstances relevant to the petition.

(f) The circuit court shall grant the petition if the circuit court finds by a preponderance of the evidence the following:

(1) The petitioner is not likely to act in a manner that is dangerous to public safety; and

(2) Granting the petition would not be contrary to the public interest.

(g) The petitioner may appeal a final order denying the petition and the review on appeal shall be de novo.

(h) A veteran may file a petition under this section no more than one (1) time every two (2) years.

(i) When the circuit court issues an order granting a petition under this section, as soon as practicable but no later than thirty (30) days after issuance of the order, the circuit clerk shall forward a copy of the order to the Department of Arkansas State Police.

History Acts 2019, No. 917, § 2.

DEPARTMENT OF ARKANSAS STATE POLICE
ARKANSAS CONCEALED HANDGUN CARRY LICENSE RULES
TABLE OF CONTENTS

CHAPTER 15. Firearms Safety Training Instructor Requirements

CHAPTER 16. Denial, suspension, or revocation of a Firearms Safety Training Instructor registration

CHAPTER 17. Firearm-Sensitive Areas

CHAPTER 18. Effective Date of these Rules

DEPARTMENT OF ARKANSAS STATE POLICE
ARKANSAS CONCEALED HANDGUN CARRY LICENSE RULES

CHAPTER 1. TITLE; AUTHORITY; SCOPE

Rule 1.0 Title
These Rules shall be known as the Arkansas Concealed Handgun Carry License Rules ("Rules").

Rule 1.1 Authority; Purpose; Scope
(a) These Rules are issued pursuant to the Director's authority under ACA § 5-73-317, ACA §§ 12-8-104 et seq., and the Arkansas Administrative Procedure Act at ACA §§ 25-15-201 et seq. The purpose of these Rules is to establish the process and procedures, in conformity with Arkansas laws, for the licensing and governance of concealed handgun carry license holders; to provide standards and guidelines to instructors who train concealed handgun carry license applicants; and to outline the process and procedures for the establishment of firearm sensitive areas.
(b) These Rules do not address federal law concerning active and retired law enforcement concealed handgun carry authorization under 18 USC § 921 and § 922.
(c) These Rules do not address certified law enforcement officers' or retired law enforcement officers' concealed handgun carry authorization under the provisions of ACA § 12-15-201 and § 12-15-202.

Rule 1.2 Definitions
Definitions are adopted as follows:

(a) "Active Duty Military" - any person serving full time in the active military service of the United States of America, including members of reserve components, under published orders for active duty or full-time training. "Active Duty Military" does not include a member who is performing active duty under a call or order for a specified period of less than thirty-one (31) calendar days;

(b) "Administrator" - the designee of the Director of the Department of Arkansas State Police;

(c) "Applicant" - any person who has submitted an application to the Department for a concealed handgun carry license and paid the statutory fees;

(d) "Application" - a form of such size and design that contains the required information and documentation enabling a person to apply for a license to carry a concealed handgun, an enhanced or enhancement to a concealed handgun carry license, renewal of a concealed handgun carry license, or transfer of a concealed handgun carry license;

(e) "Application packet" - the documentation as outlined in ASP CHCL Rule 4.2 herein;

(f) "Committed" - an overnight stay in a medical or other treatment facility, whether voluntary or involuntary;

(g) "Convicted" - a person was found guilty of or pled guilty or *nolo contendere* to a criminal offense. Unless otherwise specifically stated, a "conviction" includes offenses that have been sealed or expunged;

(h) "Crime of Violence" - any offense involving the threat of physical contact or actual physical contact or any offense involving an act or omission resulting in bodily injury. A "crime of violence" can include, but is not limited to, murder, rape, sexual assault, robbery, terroristic threatening, disorderly conduct, resisting arrest, battery, or assault;

(i) "Department" - the Department of Arkansas State Police;

(j) "Director" - the Director of the Department of Arkansas State Police;

(k) "Documentation" - information that may be required to determine the applicant's eligibility. "Documentation" includes written materials that are able to be independently verified as true and correct by the Department. For example, the most reliable "documentation" of a disposition from a court is a copy of the final disposition certified by the court clerk or the keeper of the record. Convictions that have been sealed or expunged may still disqualify an applicant from receiving a concealed handgun carry license under certain circumstances.

(l) "Duplicate License" - a license to carry a concealed handgun that is issued to a licensee to replace a previously-issued license;

(m) "Enhanced License" – the status of a concealed handgun carry license when a licensee or applicant has completed enhanced training and received an endorsement to his or her license pursuant to ACA § 5-73-322(g)(3);

(n) "Enhanced Training" - the training requirements set forth in ASP CHCL Rule 13.3 for an applicant or a licensee to qualify for an enhanced concealed handgun carry license;

(o) "Firearms Safety Training Instructor" or **"Instructor"** - any person who is registered by the Director to conduct the necessary training for a licensee to carry a concealed handgun;

(p) "Hearing Officer" - the Director of Arkansas State Police or his/her designated representative acting in issues of adjudication as outlined in the Arkansas Administrative Procedure Act;

(q) "Live-fire" – training involving the use of live ammunition, as opposed to the use of "blanks" or simunition;

(r) "Passenger Terminal of an Airport" – the ticketing area, lobby, and baggage claim of an airport. The "passenger terminal of an airport" does not include any sterile area of an airport, the passenger security screening checkpoint, and all areas beyond the security checkpoint;

(s) "Possession"- for the purposes of ACA §§ 5-73-301 et seq. and these Rules, "possession" is actual or constructive possession on or about the person, in a vehicle occupied by the licensee (including, but not limited to, areas within the passenger compartment of any vehicle, such as glove boxes or containers), or otherwise readily available for use. "Possession" also includes "carrying a handgun" as stated in ACA § 5-73-312(c).
"Possession" does not include:

 (A) For a passenger car, where the handgun is unloaded and locked in the trunk;

 (B) For any vehicle, where the handgun is unloaded and located in a space outside the passenger compartment;

 (C) For a vehicle in which a space outside the passenger compartment or a trunk does not exist, where the handgun is unloaded and in a locked container and the ammunition is physically separated from the handgun, so that both are not readily accessible to any occupant of the vehicle while the vehicle is in motion;

 (D) Placement or storage of the handgun unattended in any location, not including a locked and unattended motor vehicle in a publicly owned and maintained parking lot as permitted by law, if the licensee is not in the same room and immediate vicinity (within arm's reach) of the handgun.

(t) "Registration" - a certificate granted to an instructor permitting him or her to instruct the firearms safety training provisions outlined in these Rules;

(u) "Resident" - any person who possesses a valid Arkansas driver's license or ID card and who has established domicile as evidenced by the intent to make Arkansas his or her fixed and permanent home. It is presumed for the purposes of this definition that, when a person transfers his or her Arkansas driver's license or ID card to another state for a period of thirty (30) days or longer, the person is no longer an Arkansas resident;

(v) "Storage" - for the purposes of ACA §§ 5-73-301 et seq. and these Rules, "storage" refers to storage of a handgun in a university or college-operated student dormitory or residence hall, which is prohibited under ACA § 5-73-119(c). "Storage" means to leave a handgun unattended in any location, not including a locked and unattended motor vehicle in a publicly owned and maintained parking lot as permitted by law, for any period of time, where the licensee is not in the same room and immediate vicinity (within arm's reach) of the handgun.

(w) "Training" - the training requirements set forth in ASP CHCL Rules 13.0 and 13.1 for licensure to carry a concealed handgun.

Rule 1.3 Authority to issue license
The Director may issue a license to carry a concealed handgun to any person who meets the requirements set forth in these Rules and other applicable laws.

Rule 1.4 Term of the license
The term of the license to carry a concealed handgun is five (5) years from the date of issuance, unless the license is suspended or revoked under these Rules.

Rule 1.5 Exemptions – Authorized under other laws
A person who is exempt from licensing requirements under ACA § 5-73-304 is not bound by these Rules.

Rule 1.6 Penalty for false response or document
Submitting a false answer or false documentation with an application or in other communications with the Department shall subject the applicant to the following:
(a) Criminal penalty - a person who knowingly submits a false answer to any question on a concealed handgun carry license application, or knowingly submits a false document when applying for a concealed handgun license, upon conviction is guilty of a Class B misdemeanor; and/or
(b) Non-criminal penalty - a person who knowingly submits a false answer to any question on a concealed handgun carry license application, or knowingly submits a false document when applying for a concealed handgun license, is precluded from receiving a license and is subject to immediate revocation of his or her license if it has already been issued.

Rule 1.7 Exemptions – Military and spouse

Active Duty Member
(a) An active duty member of the United States military is not required to be a resident of Arkansas to obtain an Arkansas concealed handgun carry license if the active duty member submits documentation of his or her active duty status.
(b) The active duty member must complete the classroom portion of the concealed handgun carry training.

(c) The active duty member, or a former member who has recently received an honorable discharge, may substitute a form and a letter from his or her commanding officer, as outlined in ASP CHCL Rule 13.2, for the live-fire requirement or he or she may complete the entire concealed handgun carry training course with live-fire under the ASP-registered Concealed Handgun Carry License instructor.

(d) The active duty member shall submit with his or her initial application, and any renewal, a recent passport-style photograph in appropriate electronic format.

Spouse of Active Duty Member

(e) Any spouse of an active duty military member is not required to be a resident of Arkansas to obtain an Arkansas concealed handgun carry license if the spouse of the active duty member submits documentation of his or her spouse's active duty status.

(f) Any spouse of an active duty military member must meet the same training requirements as a regular concealed handgun carry license applicant.

(g) Any spouse of an active duty military member shall submit with his or her initial application, and any renewal, a recent passport-style photograph in appropriate electronic format.

CHAPTER 2. Application

Rule 2.0 Application design
The initial application form shall be of such size and design so as to include relevant information required by current Arkansas laws. The Director shall have the authority to design and amend the renewal, transfer, or replacement application form as he or she deems necessary.

Rule 2.1 Application availability
Applicants may apply online or obtain application forms at the Department's website or a Firearms Safety Training Instructor registered with the Arkansas State Police. Submitting an application online enables the applicant to easily check the status of his or her application and may result in faster processing.

Rule 2.2 Proper Application Packet
(a) The documentation received from an applicant shall be deemed proper and complete when it contains all the required items under Arkansas law and these Rules.

(b) In addition to the fully completed application form, the following is required:
    (1) Non-refundable license fee;
    (2) A properly completed, legible, signed waiver authorizing the Department access to the applicant's records;
    (3) At least one (1) full set of the applicant's classifiable fingerprints;

(4) Proof of the applicant's timely, successful completion of an approved firearm safety training program; and

(5) Any other information the Director may require from the applicant to determine the applicant's qualifications to hold a license under the provisions of Arkansas laws, federal laws, and these Rules.

Rule 2.3 Fees

Certain fees will be necessary for the proper processing of concealed handgun carry licensing paperwork. Those fees are set by Arkansas law or state and federal rules. An instruction sheet may be issued by the Department, which outlines proper application procedures and current fees.

CHAPTER 3. License Possession Requirements

Rule 3.0 License Usage

The concealed handgun carry license issued under these Rules shall be used solely by the licensee to whom it was issued.

Rule 3.1 Possession of license

The licensee shall carry the concealed handgun carry license, or an electronic copy in acceptable electronic format, at all times while in possession of a handgun.

Rule 3.2 Contact with law enforcement

(a) While in possession of a handgun, if a licensee is asked for identification (driver's license or personal information, such as name and date of birth) by any law enforcement officer, the licensee shall present the original license, or an electronic copy in an acceptable electronic format, for inspection, along with an official form of photo identification. The licensee shall also notify the officer that he or she holds a concealed handgun carry license and that he or she has a handgun in his or her possession.

(b) If the licensee **IS NOT in possession of a handgun**, when a law enforcement officer asks the licensee for identification (driver's license or personal information, such as name and date of birth), the licensee is not required to present the concealed handgun carry license or notify the officer that he or she holds a concealed handgun carry license.

(c) Official forms of photo identification include, but are not limited to, any of the following:

(1) Current and valid Arkansas driver's license;

(2) Current and valid military identification card; or

(3) Current and valid United States passport.

(d) Reproduced copies of the official form of photo identification shall not be accepted.

(e) Acceptable electronic format for an electronic copy of the concealed handgun carry license constitutes an electronic image produced on the person's own cellular phone or other such portable electronic device that displays all the information on a concealed handgun license as clearly as an original concealed handgun license.

Rule 3.3 Current license validity
Any law enforcement officer with access to the Arkansas Crime Information Center database may query the Arkansas driver's license of the licensee for the current validity status of the concealed handgun carry license.

CHAPTER 4. Requirements for licensure

Rule 4.0 License – Requirements
The Director of the Department shall issue a license to carry a concealed handgun if the applicant meets the eligibility criteria set forth in ACA § 5-73-308 and § 5-73-309.

Rule 4.1 Application form
The application form for a license to carry a concealed handgun shall include:
(a) The name, address, place and date of birth, race, and sex of the applicant;
(b) The driver's license number and social security number of the applicant;
(c) Any previous address of the applicant for the two (2) years preceding the date of the application;
(d) Questions related to the applicant's fitness for issuance of a concealed handgun carry license;
(e) A statement whether or not the applicant has been found guilty of a crime of violence or domestic abuse;
(f) A statement that the applicant has been furnished a copy of and has reviewed the Arkansas law relevant to concealed handgun carry licensing;
(g) A warning that a knowingly false answer to any question or the knowing submission of any false document by the applicant subjects him or her to criminal prosecution and/or precludes the applicant from receiving or retaining a license; and
(h) A statement as to whether the applicant is applying for:
    (1) A restricted license which allows the person to carry any handgun other than a semiautomatic handgun;
    (2) An unrestricted license which allows the person to carry any handgun; and/or
    (3) An enhanced license which expands the areas where a concealed handgun may be carried.

Rule 4.2 Initial Application packet and procedure
The applicant for a license to carry a concealed handgun shall submit the following items as an application packet to the Department:
(a) A properly completed application form, as described herein;
(b) A nonrefundable license fee as prescribed by law;

(c) The applicable fee(s) for state and national background checks as prescribed by law;
(d) A full set of classifiable fingerprints of the applicant;
(e) A properly completed certification of training; and
(f) A signed waiver authorizing the Department access to any medical, criminal, military, or other records concerning the applicant.
An applicant who fails to submit any of the required items listed herein will be notified of the missing items. He or she will then have thirty (30) days to submit the missing items or the application will be denied.

Rule 4.3 Application packet processing by the Department
Upon receipt of the properly completed application packet as described herein, the Department shall:
(a) Forward the full set of classifiable fingerprints of the applicant to the appropriate agencies for state and national processing;
(b) Forward notice of the person's application to the sheriff of the applicant's county of residence, and, if applicable, to the police chief of the applicant's municipality of residence, who may participate, at his or her discretion, in the process by submitting a voluntary report to the Department containing any information that he or she feels may be pertinent to the licensing of any applicant. The reporting shall be made within thirty (30) days after the date the notice was sent; and
(c) Notify the applicant of any unresolved, potentially disqualifying factor discovered in his or her criminal history. An applicant must provide the documentation or other items necessary to resolve the potentially disqualifying factor within sixty (60) days of the request by the Department or the application will be denied.

Rule 4.4 Fingerprinting for initial application
(a) In the event a legible and classifiable set of fingerprints, as determined by the Department or the Federal Bureau of Investigation, cannot be obtained, the applicant shall be contacted and shall be required to be fingerprinted again. This determination may be made prior to the submission of a fingerprint card to the FBI or after one (1) rejection of the fingerprint card.
(b) After two (2) unsuccessful fingerprint card submissions (rejections) are completed, the applicant may again pay the FBI fingerprint background check fee and submit two (2) newly-completed fingerprint cards.
(c) The Director shall determine the applicant's eligibility for licensing after successful completion of the FBI fingerprint-based check.
(d) Electronic capture of the fingerprints of the applicant on a device and in a manner approved by the Director is allowed.

Rule 4.5 Unresolved arrests
(a) If a check of the applicant's criminal records uncovers any unresolved arrest(s) that could lead to the disqualification of the applicant, the applicant shall obtain a disposition of the open charge(s). A license will not be issued

until the Department receives the final disposition or other requested information.

(b) If a check of the applicant's criminal records uncovers an unresolved felony arrest over ten (10) years old, then the applicant may obtain a letter of reference, from the county sheriff, prosecuting attorney, or circuit judge of the county where the applicant resides, which states that, to the best of his or her knowledge, the applicant is of good character and free of any felony convictions.

Rule 4.6 License – Issuance

(a) The license shall be issued within one hundred twenty (120) days after the date of receipt of a properly-completed application packet (including fingerprint cards and training certificates), as described herein. That period will be tolled pending the receipt of disposition and level or facts of any outstanding criminal charges or classifiable fingerprints for the state and national background check.

(b) The Director shall issue the license or deny the application based solely on the ground that the applicant fails to qualify under the criteria established in law and these Rules. Notice of denial shall be sent to the applicant according to these Rules.

Rule 4.7 License denial – Initial application

If the Director denies the application, he shall notify the applicant in writing, stating the grounds for denial and appeal procedures under the Arkansas Administrative Procedure Act, ACA §§ 25-15-201 et seq. The letter shall be sent via certified mail, return receipt requested.

CHAPTER 5. Renewal of license

Rule 5.0 Process for renewal of license

(a) The licensee may renew his or her license no more than ninety (90) days prior to its expiration date by submitting the following renewal packet to the Department:

(1) A completed renewal form prescribed by the Department, including a verified statement that the licensee remains qualified pursuant to the criteria specified in ACA § 5-73-308(a) and § 5-73-309;

(2) The applicable fee(s) for state and national background checks, as prescribed by law;

(3) A non-refundable renewal fee in the amount prescribed by law;

(4) A certification of training form properly completed by the licensee's Firearms Safety Training Instructor and reflecting that the licensee has successfully completed the renewal Training Course including "live-fire" within the last six (6) months as required by the Department; and

(5) A digital photograph of the licensee (if the Arkansas driver's license photo is not available) within Department standardized requirement or a release

authorization to allow the Department to obtain a qualifying digital photograph of the licensee from another source.

(b) The license shall be processed for renewal upon receipt of the items listed herein, subject to a background investigation conducted pursuant to law that does not reveal any disqualifying factor or offense or unresolved arrest which could disqualify a licensee under state or federal law.

(c) The Department will notify the applicant of any unresolved, potentially disqualifying factor discovered in his or her criminal history. An applicant must provide the documentation or other items necessary to resolve the potentially disqualifying factor within sixty (60) days of request by the Department or the application will be denied.

Rule 5.1 Renewal application - late fee

(a) A licensee who fails to properly submit a renewal application packet on or before its expiration date, but before six (6) months after the license has expired, may renew his or her license by paying a late fee as prescribed by law. Receipt of the renewal packet is determined by the receipt date of the Department.

(b) Exemption from late fee – an active duty member of the armed forces of the United States, a member of the National Guard, or a member of a reserve component of the armed forces of the United States who is on active duty outside Arkansas may renew his or her license within thirty (30) days after the person returns to Arkansas by submitting the following properly-completed renewal packet to the Department:

(1) A completed renewal application form prescribed by the Department;

(2) A verified statement that the licensee remains qualified pursuant to the criteria specified in ACA § 5-73-308(a) and § 5-73-309;

(3) A non-refundable renewal fee as prescribed by Arkansas law;

(4) The applicable fee(s) for state and national background checks, as prescribed by law;

(5) A certification or training form properly completed by the licensee's Firearms Safety Training Instructor or as allowed under ASP CHCL Rule 13.2, reflecting that the licensee's training was properly and successfully conducted;

(6) If the licensee does not hold an Arkansas driver's license, a digital photograph of the licensee; and

(7) Proof of active duty military assignment outside Arkansas on the expiration date of the license.

Rule 5.2 License expired over six (6) months

(a) A license that has been expired six (6) months or more shall be deemed "inactive". A licensee whose license has become inactive may re-apply for licensure as an initial applicant. The fees and requirements shall be the same as for an initial application.

(b) Exemption from inactive status – an active duty member of the armed forces of the United States, a member of the National Guard, or a member of a reserve component of the armed forces of the United States who is on active duty outside Arkansas may renew his or her license within thirty (30) days after the person returns to Arkansas by submitting the following renewal packet to the Department:

(1) A completed renewal application form prescribed by the Department;

(2) A verified statement that the licensee remains qualified pursuant to the criteria specified in ACA § 5-73-308(a) and ACA § 5-73-309;

(3) A non-refundable renewal fee as prescribed by Arkansas law;

(4) The applicable fee(s) for state and national background checks, as prescribed by law;

(5) A certification or training form properly completed by the licensee's Firearms Safety Training Instructor, or as allowed under ASP CHCL Rule 13.2, reflecting that the licensee's training was properly and successfully conducted;

(6) If the licensee does not hold an Arkansas driver's license, a digital photograph of the licensee; and

(7) Proof of active duty military assignment outside Arkansas on the expiration date of the license.

Rule 5.3 Renewal application denial

(a) The Director of Arkansas State Police may deny a renewal of a license upon the same grounds as for denial of an initial application for license, or for any ground for revocation listed in Arkansas law or these Rules.

(b) If the Director denies the renewal application, he shall notify the applicant in writing, stating the grounds for denial and appeal procedures under the Arkansas Administrative Procedure Act, ACA §§ 25-15-201 et seq. The letter shall be sent via certified mail, return receipt requested.

Rule 5.4 Renewal of enhanced license

An enhanced concealed handgun carry license is required to be renewed under the terms outlined in this chapter.

CHAPTER 6. Other changes to license

Rule 6.0 Replacement license

A licensee may obtain a replacement license upon submission of a properly completed replacement form and payment to the Department of a fee of:

(a) Fifteen dollars ($15.00) if the licensee is 64 years of age or younger; or

(b) Seven dollars and fifty cents ($7.50) if the licensee is 65 years of age or older.

Rule 6.1 Change of address of the licensee

(a) Within thirty (30) days after changing his or her mailing and/or permanent address, an applicant for a license or a current licensee shall notify the Director in writing of the change. Both the old and new address shall be furnished. A Department form shall be provided for that purpose.

(b) If the licensee desires a new license printed with the updated information, he or she may apply for a replacement license under ASP CHCL Rule 6.0 and destroy the old license upon receipt of the replacement license.

Rule 6.2 Change of name of the licensee
(a) Within thirty (30) days after changing his or her legal name, an applicant for a license or a current licensee shall notify the Director in writing of the change and provide documentation that officially created the change. A Department form shall be provided for that purpose.
(b) If the licensee desires a new license printed with the updated information, he or she may apply for a replacement license under ASP CHCL Rule 6.0 and destroy the old license upon receipt of the replacement license.

Rule 6.3 Death of licensee
Upon death of a licensee, the license shall be cancelled from the date of death. Written notice of the death of a licensee should be provided to the Department as soon as possible after the death.

Rule 6.4 Voluntary surrender of a license
If a licensee voluntarily surrenders his or her license to the Department in the absence of suspension or revocation proceedings, the Department will accept the license and cancel it.

Rule 6.5 Upgrade to enhanced license
A licensee may upgrade his or her basic concealed handgun carry license to an enhanced license by completion of the training described in ASP CHCL Rule 13.3, submission of a properly completed enhanced training form, and payment of the replacement fees described in ASP CHCL Rule 6.0 to the Department. A Department form shall be provided for that purpose.

CHAPTER 7. License Restrictions

Rule 7.0 Failure to comply with concealed handgun carry license restrictions
Failure to comply with the provisions of ACA §§ 5-73-301 et seq. or these Rules is a ground(s) for suspension and/or revocation of an Arkansas concealed handgun carry license.

Rule 7.1 Restrictions as to type of handgun
(a) A restricted license allows the licensee to carry concealed any legal handgun other than a semiautomatic handgun.
(b) An unrestricted license allows the licensee to carry concealed any legal handgun.

Rule 7.2 General Prohibited Places

A licensee with a non-enhanced license is barred from carrying a concealed handgun in the following places:

(a) The developed property of a public or private school, kindergarten through grade twelve (K-12), in or upon any school bus, or at a designated school bus stop, except as permitted in ACA § 5-73-119(e) [see ACA § 5-73-119(b)];

(b) The property of any private institution of higher education or a publicly supported institution of higher education, except as permitted in ACA § 5-73-322 and ACA § 5-73-119(e) [see ACA § 5-73-119(c)];

(c) Any publicly owned building or facility or on the State Capitol grounds, except as permitted in ACA § 5-73-122(a)(3) [see ACA § 5-73-122(a)(1)];

(d) The State Capitol Building or the Justice Building in Little Rock, except as permitted in ACA § 5-73-122(a)(3) [see ACA § 5-73-122(a)(2)]:

(e) On the grounds of a private university or private college, if the university or college adopts a policy expressly disallowing the carrying of a concealed handgun [see ACA § 5-73-322(c)];

(f) Any police station, sheriff's station, or Department of Arkansas State Police station [see ACA § 5-73-306(1)];

(g) Any Arkansas Highway Police Division of the Arkansas State Highway and Transportation Department facility [see ACA § 5-73-306(2)];

(h) Any building of the Arkansas State Highway and Transportation Department or onto grounds adjacent to any building of the Arkansas State Highway and Transportation Department, except as permitted in ACA § 5-73-306(3)(B) [see ACA § 5-73-306(3)];

(i) Any part of a detention facility, prison, or jail, including without limitation a parking lot owned, maintained or otherwise controlled by the Department of Correction or Department of Community Correction [see ACA § 5-73-306(4)];

(j) Any courthouse, courthouse annex, or other building owned, leased, or regularly used by a county for conducting court proceedings or housing a county office, except as permitted in ACA § 5-73-306(5)(A)-(C) [see ACA § 5-73-306(5)];

(k) Any courtroom, except as permitted in ACA § 5-73-306(6)(B) [see ACA § 5-73-306(6)];

(l) Any meeting place of the governing body of any governmental entity [see ACA § 5-73-306(7)];

(m) Any meeting of the General Assembly or a committee of the General Assembly [see ACA § 5-73-306(8)];

(n) Any state office [see ACA § 5-73-306(9)];

(o) Any athletic event not related to firearms [see ACA § 5-73-309(10)];

(p) Any portion of an establishment, except a restaurant as defined in ACA § 3-5-1202, licensed to dispense alcoholic beverages for consumption on the premises [see ACA § 5-73-306(11)];

(q) A portion of an establishment, except a restaurant as defined in ACA § 3-5-1202, where beer or light wine is consumed on the premises [see ACA § 5-73-306(12)];

(r) A school, college, community college, or university campus building or event, except as permitted in ACA § 5-73-306(13)(B) [see ACA § 5-73-306(13)];

(s) Inside the passenger terminal of any airport [see ACA § 5-73-306(14)];
(t) Any church or other place of worship, except as permitted in ACA § 5-73-306(15)(B) [see ACA § 5-73-306(15)];
(u) Any place where the carrying of a firearm is prohibited by federal law [see ACA § 5-73-306(16)];
(v) Any place where a parade or demonstration requiring a permit is being held, and the licensee is a participant in the parade or demonstration [see ACA § 5-73-306(17)];
(w) Any place at the discretion of the person or entity exercising control over the physical location, if the location posts written notice under ACA § 5-73-306(18) [see ACA § 5-73-306(18)];
(x) A place owned or operated by a private entity that prohibits the carrying of a concealed handgun, if the licensee receives written or verbal notice under ACA § 5-73-306(19) [see ACA § 5-73-306(19)]; or
(y) A posted firearm-sensitive area under ACA § 5-73-325, located at the Arkansas State Hospital, the University of Arkansas for Medical Sciences, or a collegiate athletic event [see ACA § 5-73-306(20)];

Rule 7.3 Enhanced license

An enhanced license expands the areas where a licensee may carry a concealed handgun. A current licensee or new applicant who obtains an enhanced license is exempt from the prohibitions and restrictions on carrying a concealed handgun in a publicly owned building or facility under ACA § 5-73-122 and in a prohibited place listed under ACA § 5-73-306(7)-(12), (14), (15), and (17). Those locations are listed as follows:
(a) Publicly owned buildings and facilities;
(b) State Capitol grounds and the State Capitol Building;
(c) Any meeting place of the governing body of any governmental entity;
(d) Any meeting place of the General Assembly or a committee of the General Assembly;
(e) Any state office;
(f) Athletic events;
(g) A portion of an establishment licensed to dispense alcoholic beverages for consumption on the premises;
(h) A portion of an establishment where beer or light wine is consumed on the premises;
(i) Inside the passenger terminal of an airport;
(j) Any church or other place of worship;
(k) Any place where a parade or demonstration requiring a permit is being held, even when the licensee is a participant in the parade or demonstration;
(l) The buildings and grounds of a public university, college, or community college.
Carrying a concealed firearm in the listed locations may be restricted or prohibited by other applicable law.

Rule 7.4 Enhanced Prohibited Places

A licensee with an enhanced license remains subject to other criminal prohibitions and restrictions and is barred from carrying a concealed handgun in the following places:

(a) The developed property of a public or private school, kindergarten through grade twelve (K-12), in or upon any school bus, or at a designated school bus stop, except as permitted in ACA § 5-73-119(e) [see ACA § 5-73-119(b)];

(b) The property of any private institution of higher education or a publicly supported institution of higher education, except as permitted in ACA § 5-73-322 and ACA § 5-73-119(e) [see ACA § 5-73-119(c)];

(c) Any courtroom or the location of an administrative hearing conducted by a state agency, except as permitted in ACA § 5-73-306(5) or (6) [see ACA § 5-73-122(a)(3)(D)(i)];

(d) Public school kindergarten through grade twelve (K-12), a public prekindergarten, or a public daycare facility, except as permitted in ACA § 5-73-122(a)(3)(C) [see ACA § 5-73-122(a)(3)(D)(ii)];

(e) A facility operated by the Department of Correction or the Department of Community Correction [see ACA § 5-73-122(a)(3)(D)(iii)];

(f) Any police station, sheriff's station, or Department of Arkansas State Police station [see ACA § 5-73-306(1)];

(g) Any Arkansas Highway Police Division of the Arkansas State Highway and Transportation Department facility [see ACA § 5-73-306(2)];

(h) Any building of the Arkansas State Highway and Transportation Department or onto grounds adjacent to any building of the Arkansas State Highway and Transportation Department, except as permitted in ACA § 5-73-306(3)(B) [see ACA § 5-73-306(3)];

(i) Any part of a detention facility, prison, or jail, including without limitation a parking lot owned, maintained or otherwise controlled by the Department of Correction or Department of Community Correction [see ACA § 5-73-306(4)];

(j) Any courthouse, courthouse annex, or other building owned, leased, or regularly used by a county for conducting court proceedings or housing a county office, except as permitted in ACA § 5-73-306(5)(A)-(C) [see ACA § 5-73-306(5)];

(k) Any courtroom, except as permitted in ACA § 5-73-306(6)(B) [see ACA § 5-73-306(6)];

(l) Any portion of an establishment, except a restaurant as defined in ACA § 3-5-1202, licensed to dispense alcoholic beverages for consumption on the premises, if the establishment posts written notice under ACA § 5-73-306(18) or the licensee receives written or verbal notice under ACA § 5-73-306(19) [see ACA § 5-73-306(11)];

(m) A portion of an establishment, except a restaurant as defined in ACA § 3-5-1202, where beer or light wine is consumed on the premises, if the establishment posts written notice under ACA § 5-73-306(18) or the licensee receives written or verbal notice under ACA § 5-73-306(19) [see ACA § 5-73-306(12)];

(n) A school, college, community college, or university campus building or event, except as permitted in ACA § 5-73-306(13)(B) or ACA § 5-73-322 [see ACA § 5-73-306(13)];

(o) Any church or other place of worship, if the location posts written notice under ACA § 5-73-306(18) or the licensee receives written or verbal notice under ACA § 5-73-306(19) [see ACA § 5-73-306(15)];

(p) Any place where the carrying of a firearm is prohibited by federal law [see ACA § 5-73-306(16)];

(q) Any place at the discretion of the person or entity exercising control over the physical location, if the location posts written notice under ACA § 5-73-306(18) [see ACA § 5-73-306(18)];

(r) A place owned or operated by a private entity that prohibits the carrying of a concealed handgun, if the licensee receives written or verbal notice under ACA § 5-73-306(19) [see ACA § 5-73-306(19)];

(s) A posted firearm-sensitive area under ACA § 5-73-325, located at the Arkansas State Hospital, the University of Arkansas for Medical Sciences, or a collegiate athletic event [see ACA § 5-73-306(20)];

(t) On the grounds of a private university or private college, if the university or college adopts a policy expressly disallowing the carrying of a concealed handgun [see ACA § 5-73-322(c)]; or

(u) Any location where an official meeting is being conducted in accordance with documented grievance and disciplinary procedures on the grounds of a public university, public college, or community college and is in compliance with the requirements of ACA § 5-73-322(e) [see ACA § 5-73-322(e)];

Rule 7.5 Terms of Enhanced License

(a) Once an applicant or licensee obtains the enhancement to his or her concealed handgun carry license, the enhancement will remain on his or her license until the license is revoked or becomes inactive (expiration beyond six (6) months).

(b) The enhanced license is subject to denial, suspension, and revocation on the same terms as a non-enhanced concealed handgun carry license.

(c) A licensee who completes the enhanced training course and obtains the enhanced license shall not be required to complete renewal enhanced training when he or she renews his or her license. However, if the license is ever revoked, surrendered, or becomes inactive (expiration beyond six (6) months), the former licensee will be required to complete the standard concealed handgun carry license training course and the enhanced training course to be eligible to obtain a new enhanced license.

(d) A licensee must obtain an Arkansas concealed handgun carry license to receive an enhanced license. The Department will not extend an enhanced certification to a weapons permit issued by another state; nor will enhanced or advanced weapons permits issued by other states entitle the holder to the benefits of the Arkansas enhanced license.

Rule 7.6 Enhanced License – Restrictions

(a) An enhanced license authorizes the licensee to "carry" or "possess" a concealed handgun in the buildings and on the grounds of certain locations. Possession is limited to carrying of the handgun on or about the licensee's person, in a vehicle occupied by licensee, or otherwise readily available for use. At all times, the licensee must retain the firearm in his or her immediate vicinity (within arm's reach). A licensee is not authorized to leave the handgun unattended in a separate location for safekeeping or future use, except when the handgun is placed in a locked and unattended motor vehicle in a publicly owned and maintained parking lot as permitted by law.

(b) When carrying a handgun in a location authorized by the enhanced license, the handgun must be concealed from observation so as to prevent public view. Inadvertent exposure of a handgun does not constitute a violation of this section unless the licensee repeatedly engages in careless behavior that results in exposure.

CHAPTER 8. Suspension of License

Rule 8.0 License suspension

(a) If the licensee is arrested, issued a citation, or formally charged with a crime that could disqualify the licensee from having a license, the licensee shall immediately notify the Department to the attention of the Concealed Handgun Carry Licensing Section.

(b) Any time the Department discovers that a licensee has been arrested, issued a citation, or formally charged with a crime that could disqualify the licensee from having a license, the Director may suspend a license until final disposition of the case.

(c) Notice of license suspension shall be sent to the licensee via certified mail, return receipt requested.

(d) The licensee shall be required to send the license to the Department as soon as possible after the arrest, unless the officer(s) confiscated the license at the time of arrest.

(e) The licensee shall be required to notify the Department of final disposition of the charge(s) within ten (10) days of same.

(f) If the charges are dismissed or "nol prossed," or the licensee is found "not guilty," then the license will be returned to the licensee, if it has not expired. If the license has expired for a period of less than six (6) months, then the licensee may apply for renewal of the license under these Rules.

(g) Suspension of a license is subject to the Arkansas Administrative Procedure Act, ACA §§ 25-15-201 et seq. The suspended license holder, upon his or her timely request in writing, shall be afforded an administrative hearing.

(h) The Department is required by Arkansas law to suspend the license of any licensee if so ordered by the Office of Child Support Enforcement (OCSE). The licensee will be sent notice of the suspension. The license may be reinstated (if it is still within its valid issuance period) upon full payment of the amount due to OCSE and once the Department receives official notice from OCSE to release the suspension.

(i) A licensee may apply for renewal of his or her license during a period of suspension to prevent the license from expiring or becoming inactive, however, the suspension will remain in effect until the outstanding matter is otherwise resolved.

Rule 8.1 Arrest of licensee

(a) A law enforcement officer making an arrest of a licensee for a violation of Arkansas law and/or these Rules, or any other statutory violation which could lead to revocation of a license to carry a concealed handgun, shall confiscate the license and forward it immediately to the Director.

(b) The license shall be held by the Department until a determination of the charge or violation is finalized, with the appropriate disposition of the license after the determination.

(c) If the licensee is not in possession of his or her concealed handgun carry license at the time of the arrest, the officer is not required to take possession of the license, but must forward the supporting paperwork to the Arkansas State Police, Concealed Handgun Carry Licensing Section, for further Department action on the license and retention in Department records.

(d) Any non-Arkansas concealed handgun carry license may be confiscated in a similar manner and be immediately forwarded to the Arkansas State Police, Concealed Handgun Carry Licensing Section, along with any supporting paperwork, for proper action and disposition by Department personnel.

Rule 8.2 Order of Summary Suspension

The Director may issue a written order of summary suspension of a license if it is determined that the public health, safety, or welfare requires emergency action. The suspended license holder, upon timely request in writing, shall be afforded an administrative hearing.

CHAPTER 9. Revocation of License

Rule 9.0 Revocation

(a) The Director shall revoke a concealed handgun carry license if:

(1) The licensee, at any time during the license period, becomes ineligible under the criteria set forth in state or federal law or these Rules;

(2) The Department receives notification from any law enforcement agency, court, or the licensee that a licensee has been found guilty or has pled guilty or *"nolo contendere"* to any crime involving the use of a weapon; or

(3) The Department receives notification from any law enforcement agency, court, or the licensee that a licensee has been found guilty or has pled guilty or *"nolo contendere"* to an alcohol-related offense committed while carrying a handgun.

(b) The Director may revoke a concealed handgun carry license if he or she, the Director's designee, or the county sheriff or chief of police of the applicant's place of residence executes an affidavit that the applicant has been, or is reasonably likely to be, a danger to himself or herself or others or to the community at large, as demonstrated by past patterns of behavior, participation in an incident involving unlawful violence or threats of unlawful violence, or if the applicant is under a criminal investigation.

Rule 9.1 Notice
(a) Notice of the revocation of a concealed handgun carry license shall be sent to the licensee via certified mail, return receipt requested, to the last address provided by the licensee in the Department records.
(b) An appeal from the decision to revoke a concealed handgun carry license shall be made in accordance with the appeal procedure established by the Department and the Arkansas Administrative Procedure Act, ACA §§ 25-15-201 et seq.

CHAPTER 10. Administrative Hearings

Rule 10.0 Appeal hearings
(a) In any hearing held for the purpose of affording a person the opportunity to demonstrate his or her qualifications after the denial of a license, the burden of proof shall be on the applicant.
(b) In any hearing held for the purpose of affording a person the opportunity to demonstrate his or her qualifications after a suspension or revocation of a license, the burden of proof shall be on the Department.
(c) The hearing shall be conducted in accordance with the Arkansas Administrative Procedure Act, ACA §§ 25-15-201 et seq.

Rule 10.1 Possession of license pending appeal
Upon notification of suspension or revocation, the concealed handgun carry licensee shall return the concealed handgun carry license to the Director. Any concealed handgun carry license under suspension or revocation is subject to seizure at any time by any law enforcement officer.

CHAPTER 11. Re-application after License Revocation

Rule 11.0 Re-application procedures
(a) Once a concealed handgun carry license is revoked by the Director, the former licensee shall not be eligible to apply for a concealed handgun carry license for a period of at least twenty-four (24) months from the date of revocation or other exclusion period stated in the law. After that time period expires, the applicant may reapply as a new applicant.
(b) The re-application shall be treated as an initial application by the Department.

CHAPTER 12. Honoring other states' license to carry a concealed handgun

Rule 12.0 Effect
(a) Any person in possession of a valid license to carry a concealed handgun issued by another state shall be entitled to the privileges and subject to the restrictions prescribed by Arkansas concealed handgun carry laws, federal laws, and these Rules in order to carry a concealed handgun in the State of Arkansas.
(b) Any Arkansas licensee who is present in another state has the responsibility to determine if the Arkansas Concealed Handgun Carry License is honored in that state and any requirements that may be imposed by that state.

Rule 12.1 Procedure for transfer of a license issued by another state to Arkansas
(a) Any person who becomes a resident of Arkansas and who has a valid license to carry a concealed handgun issued by another state may apply to transfer his or her license to Arkansas by submitting the following packet to the Department:
    (1) A properly completed Department transfer application form;
    (2) The person's current, original out-of-state license (if the concealed handgun carry license is contained on the driver's license of that state, then other suitable documentation as outlined by the Department will be required);
    (3) Two (2) properly completed, classifiable and legible fingerprint cards;
    (4) A nonrefundable license transfer fee as set by law; and
    (5) Any fee charged by a state or federal agency for a criminal history check.
(b) The license is valid for a period of five (5) years from the date of issuance and binds the holder to compliance with all Arkansas laws and Rules regarding the carrying of the concealed handgun.
(c) The minimum Arkansas residency requirement of ninety (90) days does not apply to applicants for a transfer of a license to carry a concealed handgun from another state.

CHAPTER 13. Training Requirement for Concealed Handgun Carry License

Rule 13.0 Training requirements upon initial application
(a) A person shall, prior to submitting an initial application for a concealed handgun carry license, successfully complete a Department approved firearm safety training program. The training must be conducted and attested to by a registered Firearms Safety Training Instructor as defined in these Rules. The program shall consist of a minimum of five (5) hours of instruction on the following topics:

(1) Administrative matters, including the application process and explanation of criteria for passing the course;
    (2) Avoiding victimization;
    (3) Laws regarding use of a handgun;
    (4) Arkansas Concealed Handgun Carry Licensing laws and Rules;
    (5) Encounters with law enforcement;
    (6) Inspection of the handgun;
    (7) Types of handguns;
    (8) Ammunition;
    (9) Cleaning and storage of a handgun;
    (10) Carrying "concealed;"
    (11) Classroom preparation for range instruction.

(b) The required training for an initial license may be completed at any time within six (6) months prior to the Department's receipt of a properly completed application packet.

(c) The applicant must successfully demonstrate proficiency with the use of a handgun on the firing range by "live-fire."

(d) An instructor may not provide his or her own training certification for his or her own Arkansas concealed handgun carry license initial application.

(e) A valid, current firearm safety training instructor registration issued by the Department may be substituted as the training requirement for an initial concealed handgun carry license.

Rule 13.1 Training requirements upon renewal of license

(a) The required training as established by the Department for renewal shall be completed at any time within six (6) months prior to the expiration of the license until six (6) months after expiration. Timely renewal is determined by the Department's receipt date of the completed renewal application packet.

(b) The applicant must successfully demonstrate proficiency with the use of a handgun on the firing range by "live-fire." Renewal training may also address updates and changes in the concealed handgun carry licensing laws and Rules.

(c) An applicant who desires to obtain an enhanced license upon renewal may substitute an enhanced training certificate for the renewal training requirement.

(d) An instructor may not provide his or her own training certification for his or her own Arkansas concealed handgun carry license renewal application; however, the instructor may substitute his or her valid, current firearms safety training instruction registration issued by the Department for the renewal training requirement.

Rule 13.2 Substitution of "live-fire" training

An active duty member of, or person who has recently been honorably discharged from, the United States Armed Forces, the National Guard, or a reserve component of the United States Armed Forces may substitute the following documentation, in a properly completed application packet, in place of the "live-fire" training requirement:

(a) A letter dated and personally signed by a commanding officer or his or her designee stating that the applicant is of good character and sound judgment;
(b) A form, as designated by the Department, showing that the applicant has met the military qualification requirements for issuance and operation of a handgun within one (1) year of the application date.
(c) A copy of the face or photograph side of a current United States Uniformed Services military identification card, if the applicant is a member of the United States Armed Forces; and
(d) A copy of the active duty orders, if the applicant is on active duty.

Rule 13.3 Training Requirements for Enhanced License

(a) The program shall consist of approximately eight (8) hours instruction – five to six (5-6) hours in-class and a maximum two (2) hours of range qualification. The Department may provide instructors with an example Syllabus for Enhanced Training to be used as a guide for its instruction. The following topics must be covered in detail as part of the in-class instruction for enhanced training:

(1) ACA §§ 5-73-101 to 325 and all significant changes to these chapters as they occur;

(2) The terms of an Enhanced License, including the rights and responsibilities of an Enhanced License holder and all locations where the carry of concealed firearms remains prohibited;

(3) Self-Defense under Arkansas law, the use of deadly physical force, the subchapter of Arkansas Code on "Justification" (ACA §§ 5-2-601 to -622), and the potential criminal penalties that may be imposed when the use of deadly physical force is not justified;

(4) Techniques for weapon retention;

(5) General civil liability for personal injury or property damage resulting from use of a firearm;

(6) Emergent situations in public locations, including the proper response to law enforcement and the duty to avoid injury to innocent bystanders;

(7) Issues related to campus carry, to include, but not be limited to:

    (A) Responsibility of the licensee to know and obey the campus's weapons policies;

    (B) Distinction between "possession" of a firearm, which is permissible, and "storage" which is not permissible; and

    (C) Requirement to carry concealed and potential penalties for violation;

(8) Other considerations for expanded carry, to include, but not be limited to:

    (A) Dangers of carrying or deploying a firearm in proximity to hazardous materials;

    (B) Possible ramifications of alcohol use while in possession of a firearm; and

(C) Identification as an Enhanced License holder in contact with law enforcement.

The Department may provide instructors with an example Syllabus for Enhanced Training to be used as a guide for its instruction.

(b) A new applicant for a concealed handgun carry license or a current licensee may apply to the Department to receive an Enhanced License. The enhanced training must be conducted and attested to by a registered Firearms Safety Training Instructor as defined in these Rules. To qualify for the Enhanced License:

(1) A new applicant must successfully complete the Department approved initial training requirements for licensure in ASP CHCL Rule 13.0 and the Department approved enhanced firearm safety training program.

(2) A current licensee must successfully complete the Department approved enhanced firearm safety training program.

(c) The required training for an Enhanced License may be completed at any time within six (6) months prior to the Department's receipt of an application for an Enhanced License, but such enhanced training is not required to be renewed.

(d) The applicant must complete a live-fire proficiency qualification and obtain a score of 35/50 or 70% overall. The instructor may permit the applicant to re-fire the course three (3) times. If the applicant fails to obtain the required score after three (3) attempts at shooting the course, the instructor must wait ninety (90) days prior to allowing the applicant attempt completion of the live-fire proficiency qualification again. The fundamentals of the live-fire course are as follows:

(1) Stage 1: 3 yard line – 20 Rounds

(A) 5 shots fired in a "one shot exercise" – 2 seconds allowed for each shot;

(B) 10 shots fired in a "two shot exercise" – 3 seconds allowed for each 2 shot sequence;

(C) 5 shots fired in 10 seconds;

(2) Stage 2: 7 yard line – 20 rounds

(A) 5 shots fired in 10 seconds

(B) 5 shots fired in 2 stages:

(i) 2 shots fired in 4 seconds;

(ii) 3 shots fired in 6 seconds;

(C) 5 shots fired in a "one shot exercise" – 3 seconds allowed for each shot;

(D) 5 shots fired in 15 seconds;

(3) Stage 3: 15 yard line – 10 rounds

(A) 5 shots fired in 2 stages:

(i) 2 shots fired in 6 seconds;

(ii) 3 shots fired in 9 seconds;

(B) 5 shots fired in 15 seconds;

(4) All shooting is from the "ready" position;

(5) The target utilized will be a B-27 target. The shooter will be scored "hit" or "miss." A successful hit will be scored if the round fired cuts the line of the 7 ring or is within the 7 ring of the B-27 target.

(e) An instructor may not provide his or her own training certification for his or her own Enhanced License; however, the instructor may substitute his or her valid, current enhanced training registration issued by the Department for the enhanced training requirement.

Rule 13.4 Waiver

A current licensee or new applicant may qualify for a waiver of a portion of the approximately eight (8) hour enhanced training course based on completion of the Arkansas basic concealed handgun carry training within the ten (10) years prior to application for an enhanced license. Documentation demonstrating the completion of the prior training must be submitted to the Department. The waiver may be applied in one of the following ways:

(a) A current licensee must complete an abbreviated course of enhanced training instruction of approximately four (4) hours of instruction and complete the live-fire proficiency qualification in Rule 13.3(d). All topics set forth in Rule 13.3(a) must be covered in the abbreviated course for the licensee to qualify for an enhanced license.

(b) A new applicant must complete a combined basic firearm safety training program and enhanced training of approximately eight (8) hours of instruction and complete the live-fire proficiency qualification in Rule 13.3(d). All topics set forth in both Rule 13.0(a) and Rule 13.3(a) must be covered in the combined course for the new applicant to qualify for an enhanced license.

CHAPTER 14. Firearms Safety Training Instructor

Rule 14.0 Purpose

(a) One of the main purposes of the Firearms Safety Training Instructor is to train and evaluate the level of competence of a prospective applicant or licensee to ensure that the person meets a basic level of knowledge, understanding, and practical operation for safe handling of a handgun.

(b) Instructors shall not certify the successful completion of the training requirements of a prospective applicant or licensee unless the person successfully meets the required standards of training.

(c) The instructor may, at the instructor's discretion, refuse to instruct or refuse to provide firearms course completion certification for any person if, in the opinion of the instructor, that person is incapable of successfully completing the required standards of training or enhanced training.

(d) Training must be conducted in person. Online training is not allowed and will not be accepted.

Rule 14.1 Maintenance of Records

(a) Instructors shall maintain all training records of every person they have instructed for the purpose of obtaining an Arkansas concealed handgun carry license for a period of not less than five (5) years from the date of training.
(b) The Department shall have audit privileges of the training records of all Firearms Safety Training Instructors.
(c) A registered Firearm Safety Training Instructor shall be present in the instruction area during any guest instructor's period to verify that the subject matter was properly covered.

Rule 14.2 Application for approval of registration
(a) The burden shall be on the Firearms Safety Training Instructor applicant for registration to bring himself or herself within the Department requirements as set out below. The applicant for registration is required to:
(1) Continuously meet the qualification requirements set forth in Arkansas law for a person to be licensed to carry a concealed handgun;
(2) Within six (6) months of application, successfully complete the examination administered by the Department. The examination shall consist of the provisions of ACA §§ 5-73-101 et seq., federal firearms laws, enhanced training topics, and these Rules;
(3) Hold a firearms instructor training certificate from a department recognized instruction course;
(4) Offer enhanced training; and
(5) Submit:
(A) A properly completed registration application;
(B) The background check fees required for state and national background checks; and
(C) One (1) set of legible, classifiable fingerprints, however the requirement for fingerprints is waived if the applicant holds a current and valid Arkansas Concealed Handgun Carry License.
(b) Department recognized firearms instructor training certificates include:
(1) Firearm instructor's certificate issued by the Arkansas Law Enforcement Standards and Training Commission;
(2) Completion of a Certified Pistol Instructor Course that is recognized by the Department and completion of a Range Officer Safety Course that is recognized by the Department; or
(3) Firearm instructor's certification issued by a federal law enforcement or military agency.
(c) The Director shall require applicants for registration as instructors to demonstrate their qualifications by examination. The examinations are given in Little Rock at the Arkansas State Police Headquarters and only with prior approval.
(d) The Director may, at his or her discretion, approve an application for registration for a person who fails to meet the qualifications as outlined in this Rule, if it is determined that the applicant is qualified by experience, education, etc. The registration applicant will still be required to successfully complete the examination administered by the Department.

(e) Instructors are not required to obtain an Arkansas concealed handgun carry license, although it is recommended.

(f) In the event the applicant is denied, the Director shall promptly notify the applicant of his or her decision in writing, via certified mail, return receipt requested, stating the reason for the denial.

14.3 Approval to teach Enhanced Training

(a) ACA § 5-73-322(g)(2)(A)(iii) requires that enhanced training be offered by all training instructors and at all concealed carry training courses. Enhanced training is a separate class from the class required to obtain an initial, non-enhanced concealed handgun carry license. Instructors are only required to teach enhanced training to students who desire an enhanced license. However, all instructors and entities that offer concealed carry training classes must also offer enhanced training classes.

(b) All instructors who have a current registration as of January 1, 2018 must successfully complete an exam administered by the Department covering the updated provisions of ACA §§ 5-73-101 et seq., federal firearms laws, the enhanced training topics, and these Rules to be approved to offer enhanced training. If an instructor fails to successfully complete the exam by January 1, 2020, his or her registration will be revoked.

(c) The enhanced training offered by the instructor must consist of approximately eight (8) hours – five to six (5-6) hours in-class and maximum two (2) hours live-fire. The instructor must cover the topics contained in ASP CHCL Rule 13.3. Failure to comply with these requirements could result in the rejection of the instructor's students' training certificates and/or suspension or revocation of the registration.

(d) Instructors may conduct combined or abbreviated enhanced training courses as described in Rule 13.4 for applicants who qualify for a waiver. Instructors must require the applicant to demonstrate proof of completion of basic concealed handgun carry training completed within the ten (10) years prior to conducting the abbreviated course.

CHAPTER 15. Firearms Safety Training Instructor Requirements

Rule 15.0 Training of Applicants

(a) The required minimum standards for the firearm safety training course for an initial concealed handgun carry license, renewal license, or Enhanced License shall be a course of instruction developed, prescribed, and acceptable to the Director and shall include utilizing "LIVE" ammunition and firing.

(b) The applicant must successfully demonstrate proficiency with the use of a handgun on the firing range.

(c) The Director shall not accept the training certificate of an applicant if the instructor did not hold a valid instructor registration with the Department at the time the training took place.

Rule 15.1 Administration of firearms safety training instruction

(a) An instructor shall at all times legally operate in accordance with all Federal, State, County, and City laws and ordinances.

(b) If the instructor ceases to be an instructor for any reason whatsoever, the Director shall be notified, in writing, of the cessation within five (5) calendar days and, if requested, provide all records to the Director.

(c) An instructor, authorized to conduct a training course required by these Rules, shall check the application of a student for completeness, accuracy, and legibility. This requirement does not apply if the student has submitted or will submit an electronic application to the Department.

Rule 15.2 Instructor Change of Address

An instructor or applicant for instructor registration shall notify the Department in writing within thirty (30) calendar days of any change in his or her name, address, electronic mail address (if any), or telephone number.

Rule 15.3 Instructor – Other requirements

(a) An instructor must include the registration number assigned to him or her by the Director on all matters of advertising for teaching Arkansas Concealed Handgun Carry License classes or offering services as a Firearms Safety Training Instructor registered with the Department. Advertising includes print, electronic or social media, such as Facebook, twitter, linkedin, etc. The instructor is not required to include the registration number on each posting from a social media account, so long as the posting is linked to account of the instructor with the registration number.

(b) An instructor may not use the Arkansas State Police star or indicate any other association with the Arkansas State Police other than they are registered with the Arkansas State Police as an Arkansas Concealed Handgun Carry License Firearms Safety Training Instructor.

(c) An instructor may not conduct any business as a registered Arkansas Concealed Handgun Carry License Firearms Safety Training Instructor under a name other than what is shown on his or her current registration on file with the Department.

Rule 15.4 Death of a registered instructor

Upon the death of a registered instructor, the registration shall be cancelled from the date of death. Written notice of the death of a registered instructor should be provided to the Department as soon as possible.

Rule 15.5 Voluntary surrender of a registration

If a registrant voluntarily surrenders his or her registration in writing to the Department in the absence of suspension or revocation proceedings, the Department will accept the registration and cancel it.

Rule 15.6 Notification of Department of arrest of a registrant

If a registrant is arrested, issued a citation, or formally charged with a crime or violation of Arkansas law and/or these Rules which could lead to revocation of a license to carry a concealed handgun, the registrant shall promptly notify the Department in writing.

CHAPTER 16. Denial, suspension, or revocation of a Firearms Safety Training Instructor registration

Rule 16.0 Grounds for denial, suspension, or revocation of a Firearms Safety Training Instructor registration

The Director has the authority to:

(a) Deny the application for registration under provisions of state or federal law and these Rules; or

(b) Suspend or revoke the firearms safety training instructor registration of any instructor who has qualified under the provisions of Arkansas law and these Rules, if it is determined that the applicant or instructor has:

(1) Practiced fraud, deceit, or misrepresentation;

(2) Made a material misstatement in the application for registration as a firearms safety training instructor;

(3) Demonstrated incompetence or untrustworthiness in his or her actions;

(4) Failed to comply with the provisions of Arkansas law and/or these Rules;

(5) Committed any act which, if committed by a licensee, would subject the concealed handgun carry licensee to denial, suspension, or revocation;

(6) Repeatedly failed to check the non-electronic applications of trainees for completeness, accuracy, and legibility;

(7) Not at all times legally operated in accordance with these Rules, and with all Federal, State, County, and City laws and ordinances;

(8) Not at all times maintained a current and valid Firearms Safety Training Instructor registration on file with the Department as required in these Rules;

(9) Been the subject of a request on file with the Department from the Office of Child Support Enforcement to suspend the registration; or

(10) Otherwise becomes ineligible to hold a concealed handgun carry license.

Rule 16.1 Appeal of the denial, suspension, or revocation of a Firearms Safety Training Instructor registration

(a) Upon the denial, suspension, or revocation of registration of a Firearm Safety Training Instructor, the Instructor shall be afforded the opportunity for an administrative hearing. The Instructor shall be sent notice via certified mail, return receipt requested and be advised in writing of his or her appeal rights.

(b) For denial of a Firearms Safety Training Instructor registration, the burden of proof in administrative proceedings shall be on the applicant for registration.

(c) For suspension or revocation of an existing Firearms Safety Training Instructor registration, the burden of proof in administrative proceedings shall be on the Department.

CHAPTER 17. Firearm-Sensitive Areas

Rule 17.0 Posted firearm-sensitive areas - Restriction
All concealed handgun carry licensees, including those with an Enhanced License, are barred from carrying a concealed handgun into Department approved, posted firearm-sensitive areas located at the Arkansas State Hospital, the University of Arkansas for Medical Sciences, or a collegiate athletic event.

Rule 17.1 Establishment of a firearm-sensitive area – Security Plan
The Arkansas State Hospital, the University of Arkansas for Medical Sciences, or any institution of higher education that hosts or sponsors a collegiate athletic event may designate certain areas "firearm-sensitive," where possession of a concealed handgun by a licensee is prohibited. To obtain approval for the designation of a "firearm-sensitive area" the entity must:
(a) Submit a security plan to the Regulatory Division of the Department, including the following information:
    (1) Total projected attendance/capacity;
    (2) Number of entrances and exits;
    (3) Number of on-site private security personnel;
    (4) Number of on-site law enforcement officers
    (5) Number of on-site first responders;
    (6) Location of parking areas and number of motor vehicles projected to use the parking areas;
    (7) Routes for emergency vehicles;
    (8) Locations of all restrooms, stairs, and elevators;
    (9) Evacuation procedures;
    (10) Security communication protocol;
    (11) Location of emergency vehicles;
    (12) Public communication protocol;
    (13) Bomb threat and active shooter procedures; and
    (14) Corresponding security measures.
(b) Indicate the area(s) and/or event(s) to be designated "firearm-sensitive."
(c) State whether the area will be designated "firearm-sensitive" at all times, or if only on certain dates and times, list the dates, times, and purposes for which the area will be designated "firearm-sensitive."
(d) List the name, title, telephone number, address, and email for the entity's preferred contact.
(e) The security plan may be submitted annually, or no later than five (5) days before a scheduled collegiate athletic event.

(f) If the security plan is submitted for a scheduled collegiate athletic event, the Department will approve or disapprove the plan within seventy-two (72) hours of receipt of the security plan.

(g) If the security plan is submitted annually, the Department will approve or disapprove the plan within ten (10) business days.

(h) Once the security plan has been approved, the entity shall post a notification at all firearm-sensitive areas that possession of a concealed handgun is prohibited.

CHAPTER 18. Effective Date of these Rules

Rule 18.0 Effective date
These Rules shall be effective on and after June 25, 2018.
****

Weapons – Possession and Use Generally

<u>Arkansas Code §5-73-101. Definitions.</u>
As used in this chapter:
(1) "Blasting agent" means any material or mixture consisting of fuel and oxidizer intended for blasting if the finished product as mixed for use or shipment cannot be detonated by means of a No. 8 test blasting cap when unconfined;
(2) "Collegiate athletic event" means a sporting or athletic contest, event, or practice of an individual or team of individuals in which one (1) or more individuals or a team of individuals sponsored by, funded by, represented by, or associated with a public or private university, college, or community college competes against themselves or another individual or team of individuals;
(3) "Contraband" means any explosive material that was used with the knowledge and consent of the owner to facilitate a violation of this subchapter, as well as any explosive material possessed under circumstances prohibited by law;
(4) "Destructive device" means:
  (A) Any of the following:
    (i) Any explosive, incendiary, or poison gas;
    (ii) Bomb;
    (iii) Grenade;
    (iv) Rocket having a propellant charge of more than four ounces (4 oz.);
    (v) Missile having an explosive or incendiary charge of more than one-quarter ounce (.25 oz.);
    (vi) Mine; or
    (vii) Similar device; and
  (B) Any combination of parts either designed or intended for use in converting any device into a destructive device as defined in subdivision (4)(A) of this section and from which a destructive device may be readily assembled for use as a weapon;
(5) (A) "Detonator" means any device containing any initiating or primary explosive that is used for initiating detonation.
  (B) A detonator may not contain more than ten grams (10g) of total explosives by weight, excluding ignition or delay charges, and may include, without limitation, electric blasting caps of instantaneous and delay types, blasting caps for use with safety fuses, detonating cord delay connectors, and noninstantaneous and delay blasting caps that use detonating cord, shock tube, or any other replacement for electric leg wires;
(6) "Distribute" means to sell, issue, give, transfer, or otherwise dispose of explosive material;
(7) "Explosive material" means an explosive, blasting agent, or detonator;
(8) (A) "Explosive" means any chemical compound mixture or device, the primary or common purpose of which is to function by explosion.
  (B) "Explosive" includes, without limitation:
    (i) Dynamite and any other high explosive;

(ii) Black powder;
(iii) Pellet powder;
(iv) An initiating explosive;
(v) A detonator;
(vi) A safety fuse;
(vii) A squib;
(viii) A detonating cord;
(ix) An igniter cord;
(x) An igniter;
(xi) Any material determined to be within the scope of 18 U.S.C. § 841 et seq.; and
(xii) Any material classified as an explosive other than consumer fireworks, 1.4 (Class C, Common), by the hazardous materials regulations of the United States Department of Transportation;
(9) "Instrument of crime" means anything manifestly designed, made, adapted, or commonly used for a criminal purpose;
(10) "Minor" means any person under eighteen (18) years of age; and
(11) "Violent felony conviction" means a conviction for any felony offense against the person which is codified in § 5-10-101 et seq., § 5-11-101 et seq., § 5-12-101 et seq., § 5-13-201 et seq., § 5-13-301 et seq., § 5-14-101 et seq., and § 5-14-201 et seq., or any other offense containing as an element of the offense one (1) of the following:
 (A) The use of physical force;
 (B) The use or threatened use of serious physical force;
 (C) The infliction of physical harm; or
 (D) The creation of a substantial risk of serious physical harm.
History Acts 1975, No. 280, § 3101; A.S.A. 1947, § 41-3101; Acts 2001, No. 1430, § 1; 2005, No. 1226, § 1; 2017, No. 859, § 1.

§5-73-102. Possessing instrument of crime.
(a) A person commits the offense of possessing an instrument of crime if he or she possesses any instrument of crime with a purpose to employ it criminally.
(b) Possessing an instrument of crime is a Class A misdemeanor.
History Acts 1975, No. 280, § 3102; A.S.A. 1947, § 41-3102.

§5-73-103. Possession of firearms by certain persons.
(a) Except as provided in subsection (d) of this section or unless authorized by and subject to such conditions as prescribed by the Governor, or his or her designee, or the United States Bureau of Alcohol, Tobacco, Firearms, and Explosives, or other bureau or office designated by the United States Department of Justice, no person shall possess or own any firearm who has been:
 (1) Convicted of a felony;
 (2) Adjudicated mentally ill; or
 (3) Committed involuntarily to any mental institution.
(b) (1) Except as provided in subdivisions (b)(2) and (3) of this section, a determination by a jury or a court that a person committed a felony constitutes

a conviction for purposes of subsection (a) of this section even though the court suspended imposition of sentence or placed the defendant on probation.

(2) Subdivision (b)(1) of this section does not apply to a person whose case was dismissed and expunged under § 16-93-301 et seq. or § 16-98-303(g).

(3) The determination by the jury or court that the person committed a felony does not constitute a conviction for purposes of subsection (a) of this section if the person is subsequently granted a pardon explicitly restoring the ability to possess a firearm.

(c) (1) A person who violates this section commits a Class B felony if:

(A) The person has a prior violent felony conviction;

(B) The person's current possession of a firearm involves the commission of another crime; or

(C) The person has been previously convicted under this section or a similar provision from another jurisdiction.

(2) A person who violates this section commits a Class D felony if he or she has been previously convicted of a felony and his or her present conduct or the prior felony conviction does not fall within subdivision (c)(1) of this section.

(3) Otherwise, the person commits a Class A misdemeanor.

(d) The Governor may restore without granting a pardon the right of a convicted felon or an adjudicated delinquent to own and possess a firearm upon the recommendation of the chief law enforcement officer in the jurisdiction in which the person resides, so long as the underlying felony or delinquency adjudication:

(1) Did not involve the use of a weapon; and

(2) Occurred more than eight (8) years ago.

History Acts 1975, No. 280, § 3103; 1977, No. 360, § 18; A.S.A. 1947, § 41-3103; Acts 1987, No. 74, § 1; 1994 (2nd Ex. Sess.), No. 63, § 1; 1995, No. 595, § 1; 1995, No. 1325, § 1; 2001, No. 1429, § 1; 2009, No. 1491, § 1.

§5-73-104. Criminal use of prohibited weapons.

(a) A person commits the offense of criminal use of prohibited weapons if, except as authorized by law, he or she knowingly uses, possesses, makes, repairs, sells, or otherwise deals in any:

(1) Bomb;

(2) Metal knuckles; or

(3) Other implement for the infliction of serious physical injury or death that serves no lawful purpose.

(b) This section does not apply if the person uses, possesses, makes, repairs, sells, or otherwise deals in an item described in this section that is in compliance with the National Firearms Act, 26 U.S.C. §§ 5801 -- 5861, or other applicable federal law, as either existed on January 1, 2019.

(c) It is a defense to prosecution under this section that:

(1) The defendant was a law enforcement officer, prosecuting attorney, deputy prosecuting attorney, prison guard, or member of the United States Armed Forces acting in the course and scope of his or her duty at the time he or she used or possessed the prohibited weapon; or

(2) The defendant used, possessed, made, repaired, sold, or otherwise dealt in any article enumerated in subsection (a) of this section under circumstances negating any likelihood that the weapon could be used as a weapon.

(d) (1) Criminal use of prohibited weapons is a Class B felony if the weapon is a bomb.

(2) Criminal use of prohibited weapons is a Class A misdemeanor if the offense is possession of metal knuckles.

(3) Otherwise, criminal use of prohibited weapons is a Class D felony.

History Acts 1975, No. 280, § 3104; A.S.A. 1947, § 41-3104; Acts 1993, No. 1189, § 7; 2005, No. 1994, § 438; 2011, No. 161, § 1; 2013, No. 539, § 1; 2019, No. 495, § 1; 2019, No. 1051, § 1.

§5-73-105. Legitimate manufacture, repair, and transportation of prohibited weapons.

Section 5-73-104 shall not be construed to prohibit the manufacture, repair, transportation, or sale of the weapons enumerated in § 5-73-104 to or for an authorized representative of:

(1) The armed forces; or

(2) Any law enforcement agency.

History Acts 1975, No. 280, § 3105; A.S.A. 1947, § 41-3105.

§5-73-106. Defacing a firearm.

(a) A person commits the offense of defacing a firearm if he or she knowingly removes, defaces, mars, covers, alters, or destroys the manufacturer's serial number or identification mark of a firearm.

(b) Defacing a firearm is a Class D felony.

History Acts 1975, No. 280, § 3106; A.S.A. 1947, § 41-3106.

§5-73-107. Possession of a defaced firearm.

(a) A person commits the offense of possession of a defaced firearm if he or she knowingly possesses a firearm with a manufacturer's serial number or other identification mark required by law that has been removed, defaced, marred, altered, or destroyed.

(b) It is a defense to a prosecution under this section that:

(1) The person reported the possession to the police or other governmental agency prior to arrest or the issuance of an arrest warrant or summons; or

(2) The firearm was manufactured prior to January 1, 1968.

(c) (1) Possession of a defaced firearm is a Class D felony.

(2) However, possession of a defaced firearm is a Class A misdemeanor if the manufacturer's serial number or other identification mark required by law is merely covered or obstructed, but still retrievable.

History Acts 1975, No. 280, § 3107; A.S.A. 1947, § 41-3107; Acts 1995, No. 1202, § 1; 2017, No. 73, § 1.

§5-73-108. Criminal acts involving explosives.

(a) (1) A person commits the offense of criminal possession of explosive material or a destructive device if the person:

(A) Sells, possesses, manufactures, transfers, or transports explosive material or a destructive device; and

(B) Either:

(i) Has the purpose of using that explosive material or destructive device to commit an offense; or

(ii) Knows or should know that another person intends to use that explosive material or destructive device to commit an offense.

(2) Criminal possession of explosive material or a destructive device is a Class B felony.

(b) (1) A person commits the offense of criminal distribution of explosive material if he or she knowingly distributes explosive material to any individual who:

(A) Has pleaded guilty or nolo contendere to or been found guilty of a crime in state or federal court punishable by imprisonment for a term exceeding one (1) year;

(B) Is a fugitive from justice;

(C) Is an unlawful user of or addicted to any controlled substance;

(D) Has been adjudicated as having a mental disease or defect or has been committed to an institution or residential treatment facility because of a mental disease or defect;

(E) Is under twenty-one (21) years of age;

(F) Is an alien, other than an alien who is:

(i) Lawfully admitted for permanent residence as defined in 8 U.S.C. § 1101(a)(20), as it existed on January 1, 2009;

(ii) In lawful nonimmigrant status, a refugee admitted under 8 U.S.C. § 1157, as it existed on January 1, 2009, or in asylum status under 8 U.S.C. § 1158, as it existed on January 1, 2009, and either:

(a) A foreign law enforcement officer of a friendly foreign government, as determined by the United States Secretary of State under 18 U.S.C. § 842, entering the United States on official law enforcement business, and the distribution of explosive material is in furtherance of this official law enforcement business; or

(b) A person having the power to direct or cause the direction of the management and policies of a corporation, partnership, or association licensed under 18 U.S.C. § 843, as it existed on January 1, 2009, and the distribution of explosive material is in furtherance of the person's power;

(iii) A member of a North Atlantic Treaty Organization or other friendly foreign military force, as determined by the United States Attorney General in consultation with the United States Secretary of Defense under 18 U.S.C. § 842, who is present in the United States under military orders for training or other military purpose authorized by the United States, and the distribution of explosive material is in furtherance of the military orders for training or authorized military purpose; or

(iv) Lawfully present in the United States in cooperation with the Director of the Central Intelligence Agency, and the distribution of explosive material is in furtherance of the cooperation;

(G) Has been dishonorably discharged from any branch of the United States Armed Forces; or

(H) Has renounced his or her United States citizenship.

(2) Criminal distribution of explosive material is a Class C felony.

(c) (1) A person commits the offense of possession of stolen explosive material if he or she:

(A) Receives, possesses, transports, ships, conceals, stores, barters, sells, disposes of, or pledges or accepts as security for a loan any stolen explosive materials; and

(B) Knows or has reasonable cause to believe that the explosive material was stolen.

(2) Possession of stolen explosive material is a Class C felony.

(d) (1) A person commits the offense of unlawful receipt or possession of an explosive material if the person receives or possesses explosive material and:

(A) Has pleaded guilty or nolo contendere to or has been found guilty in any state or federal court of a crime punishable by imprisonment for a term exceeding one (1) year;

(B) Is a fugitive from justice;

(C) Is an unlawful user of or addicted to any controlled substance;

(D) Has been adjudicated to have a mental disease or defect or has been committed to an institution or residential treatment facility because of a mental disease or defect;

(E) Is under twenty-one (21) years of age;

(F) Is an alien, other than an alien who is:

(i) Lawfully admitted for permanent residence as defined in 8 U.S.C. § 1101(a)(20), as it existed on January 1, 2009; or

(ii) In lawful nonimmigrant status, a refugee admitted under 8 U.S.C. § 1157, as it existed on January 1, 2009, or in asylum status under 8 U.S.C. § 1158, as it existed on January 1, 2009, and either:

(a) A foreign law enforcement officer of a friendly foreign government, as determined by the United States Secretary of State under 18 U.S.C. § 842, entering the United States on official law enforcement business, and the receipt or possession of the explosive material is in furtherance of this official law enforcement business; or

(b) A person having the power to direct or cause the direction of the management and policies of a corporation, partnership, or association licensed under 18 U.S.C. § 843, as it existed on January 1, 2009, and the receipt or possession of the explosive material is in furtherance of the person's power;

(iii) A member of a North Atlantic Treaty Organization or other friendly foreign military force, as determined by the United States Attorney General in consultation with the United States Secretary of Defense under 18 U.S.C. § 842, who is present in the United States under military orders for training or other military purpose authorized by the United States, and the receipt or possession of the explosive material is in furtherance of the military orders for training or authorized military purpose; or

(iv) Lawfully present in the United States in cooperation with the Director of the Central Intelligence Agency, and the receipt or possession of the explosive material is in furtherance of the cooperation;

(G) Has been dishonorably discharged from any branch of the United States Armed Forces; or

(H) Has renounced his or her United States citizenship.

(2) Unlawful receipt or possession of explosive material is a Class C felony.

(3) It is a defense to prosecution under this subsection if at the time of the receiving or possessing the explosive material the person was acting within the scope of his or her employment with a business authorized to use explosive material.

(e) It is a Class A misdemeanor for any person to store any explosive material in a manner not in conformity with the Arkansas Fire Prevention Code.

(f) A person who commits theft of any explosive material with the purpose to cause harm to a person or property is guilty of a Class B felony.

(g) Any explosive material determined to be contraband is subject to seizure by a law enforcement officer and to being destroyed in conformity with the Arkansas Fire Prevention Code.

(h) As used in this section, "alien" means a person who is not a citizen or national of the United States.

History Acts 1975, No. 280, § 3108; A.S.A. 1947, § 41-3108; Acts 2005, No. 1226, § 2; 2006 (1st Ex. Sess.), No. 14, § 1; 2009, No. 339, § 1; 2011, No. 1120, § 14.

§5-73-109. Furnishing a deadly weapon to a minor.

(a) A person commits the offense of furnishing a deadly weapon to a minor if he or she sells, barters, leases, gives, rents, or otherwise furnishes a firearm or other deadly weapon to a minor without the consent of a parent, guardian, or other person responsible for general supervision of the minor's welfare.

(b) (1) Furnishing a deadly weapon to a minor is a Class A misdemeanor.

(2) However, furnishing a deadly weapon to a minor is a Class B felony if the deadly weapon is:

(A) A handgun;

(B) An explosive or incendiary device, as defined in § 5-71-301;

(C) Metal knuckles;

(D) A defaced firearm, as described in § 5-73-107; or

(E) Another implement for the infliction of serious physical injury or death that serves no lawful purpose.

History Acts 1975, No. 280, § 3109; A.S.A., 1947, § 41-3109; Acts 1994 (2nd Ex. Sess.), No. 45, § 1; 2019, No. 495, § 2; 2019, No. 1051, § 2.

§5-73-110. Disarming minors and mentally defective or mentally irresponsible persons -- Disposition of property seized.

(a) Subject to constitutional limitation, nothing in this section and §§ 5-73-101 -- 5-73-109 shall be construed to prohibit a law enforcement officer from disarming, without arresting, a minor or person who reasonably appears to be mentally defective or otherwise mentally irresponsible when that person is in possession of a deadly weapon.

(b) Property seized under subsection (a) of this section shall be:

(1) Held for seventy-two (72) hours by the law enforcement agency employing the law enforcement officer who seized the property; and

(2) After the seventy-two-hour hold and upon request and presentation of valid proof of ownership, returned to the:

(A) Owner, if he or she is eighteen (18) years of age or older and may lawfully possess the property; or

(B) Parent or legal guardian of the owner, if the owner is a minor and the parent or legal guardian may lawfully possess the property.

History Acts 1975, No. 280, § 3110; A.S.A. 1947, § 41-3110; Acts 2015, No. 688, § 1.

§5-73-111. Unlawful procurement of a firearm.

(a) As used in this section:

(1) "Ammunition" means any cartridge, shell, or projectile designed for use in a firearm;

(2) "False information" means information that portrays an unlawful transaction as lawful or a lawful transaction as unlawful;

(3) "Licensed dealer" means a person who is licensed under 18 U.S.C. § 923, as it existed on January 1, 2013, to engage in the business of dealing in firearms; and

(4) "Private seller" means a person other than a licensed dealer who sells or offers for sale a firearm or ammunition.

(b) A person commits the offense of unlawful procurement of a firearm or ammunition if he or she knowingly:

(1) Solicits, persuades, encourages, or entices a licensed dealer or private seller to transfer a firearm or ammunition under unlawful circumstances; or

(2) Provides false information to a licensed dealer or private seller with a purpose to deceive the licensed dealer or private seller concerning the lawfulness of a transfer of a firearm or ammunition.

(c) It is a defense to prosecution under this section if the person is:

(1) A law enforcement officer acting in his or her official capacity; or

(2) Acting at the direction of a law enforcement officer.

(d) Unlawful procurement of a firearm or ammunition is a Class D felony.

History Acts 2013, No. 507, § 1.

§5-73-112. Certification by a chief law enforcement officer regarding receipt or manufacture of a firearm.

(a) As used in this section:

(1) "Certification" means the participation and assent of the chief law enforcement officer or his or her designee necessary under federal law for the approval of an application to transfer or manufacture a firearm; and

(2) "Firearm" means the same as defined in § 5845(a) of the National Firearms Act, 26 U.S.C. § 5801 et seq. as it existed on January 1, 2015.

(b) (1) When certification by the chief law enforcement officer of a jurisdiction is required by federal law or regulation for the transfer or manufacture of a firearm within fifteen (15) days of receipt of a request for certification, the chief law enforcement officer or his or her designee shall provide the certification if the applicant is not prohibited by law from receiving or manufacturing the firearm or is not the subject of a proceeding that could result in the applicant's being prohibited by law from receiving or manufacturing the firearm.

(2) If the applicant is prohibited by law from receiving or manufacturing the firearm or is the subject of a proceeding that could result in a prohibition against his or her receiving or manufacturing the firearm, the chief law enforcement officer or his or her designee shall provide written notification to the applicant that states the reasons for his or her findings and that the certification is denied.

(c) (1) An applicant whose request for certification is denied may appeal the denial to the circuit court where the applicant resides.

(2) The circuit court shall review the denial de novo.

(3) If the circuit court finds that the applicant is not prohibited by law from receiving or manufacturing the firearm or is not the subject of a proceeding that could result in a prohibition against his or her receiving or manufacturing the firearm, the circuit court shall order the chief law enforcement officer to issue the certification to the applicant.

(d) Except as provided in subdivision (c)(3) of this section, the chief law enforcement officer of a jurisdiction and his or her employees who act in good faith are immune from civil liability arising from any act or omission in making a certification under this section.

History Acts 2015, No. 720, § 1.

§5-73-113 -- 5-73-118. [Reserved.]

§5-73-119. Handguns -- Possession by minor or possession on school property.

(a) (1) No person in this state under eighteen (18) years of age shall possess a handgun.

(2) (A) A violation of subdivision (a)(1) of this section is a Class A misdemeanor.

(B) A violation of subdivision (a)(1) of this section is a Class D felony if the person has previously:

(i) Been adjudicated delinquent for a violation of subdivision (a)(1) of this section;

(ii) Been adjudicated delinquent for any offense that would be a felony if committed by an adult; or

(iii) Pleaded guilty or nolo contendere to or been found guilty of a felony in circuit court while under eighteen (18) years of age.

(b) (1) No person in this state shall possess a firearm:

(A) Upon the developed property of a public or private school, kindergarten through grade twelve (K-12);

(B) In or upon any school bus; or

(C) At a designated bus stop as identified on the route list published by a school district each year.

(2) (A) A violation of subdivision (b)(1) of this section is a Class D felony.

(B) No sentence imposed for a violation of subdivision (b)(1) of this section shall be suspended or probated or treated as a first offense under § 16-93-301 et seq.

(c) (1) Except as provided in § 5-73-322, a person in this state shall not possess a handgun upon the property of any private institution of higher education or a publicly supported institution of higher education in this state on or about his or her person, in a vehicle occupied by him or her, or otherwise readily available for use with a purpose to employ the handgun as a weapon against a person.

(2) A violation of subdivision (c)(1) of this section is a Class D felony.

(d) "Handgun" means a firearm capable of firing rimfire ammunition or centerfire ammunition and designed or constructed to be fired with one (1) hand.

(e) It is permissible to carry a handgun under this section if at the time of the act of possessing a handgun or firearm:

(1) The person is in his or her own dwelling or place of business or on property in which he or she has a possessory or proprietary interest, except upon the property of a public or private institution of higher learning;

(2) The person is a law enforcement officer, correctional officer, or member of the armed forces acting in the course and scope of his or her official duties;

(3) The person is assisting a law enforcement officer, correctional officer, or member of the armed forces acting in the course and scope of his or her official duties pursuant to the direction or request of the law enforcement officer, correctional officer, or member of the armed forces;

(4) The person is a registered commissioned security guard acting in the course and scope of his or her duties;

(5) The person is hunting game with a handgun or firearm that may be hunted with a handgun or firearm under the rules and regulations of the Arkansas State Game and Fish Commission or is en route to or from a hunting area for the purpose of hunting game with a handgun or firearm;

(6) (A) The person is a certified law enforcement officer, either on-duty or off-duty.

(B) If the person is an off-duty law enforcement officer, he or she may be required by a public school or publicly supported institution of higher education to be in physical possession of a valid identification identifying the person as a law enforcement officer;

(7) The person is on a journey beyond the county in which the person lives, unless the person is eighteen (18) years of age or less;

(8) The person is participating in a certified hunting safety course sponsored by the commission or a firearm safety course recognized and approved by the commission or by a state or national nonprofit organization qualified and experienced in firearm safety;

(9) The person is participating in a school-approved educational course or sporting activity involving the use of firearms;

(10) The person is a minor engaged in lawful marksmanship competition or practice or other lawful recreational shooting under the supervision of his or

her parent, legal guardian, or other person twenty-one (21) years of age or older standing in loco parentis or is traveling to or from a lawful marksmanship competition or practice or other lawful recreational shooting with an unloaded handgun or firearm accompanied by his or her parent, legal guardian, or other person twenty-one (21) years of age or older standing in loco parentis;

(11) The person has a license to carry a concealed handgun under § 5-73-301 et seq. and is carrying a concealed handgun on the developed property of:

(A) A kindergarten through grade twelve (K-12) private school operated by a church or other place of worship that:

(i) Is located on the developed property of the kindergarten through grade twelve (K-12) private school;

(ii) Allows the person to carry a concealed handgun into the church or other place of worship under § 5-73-306; and

(iii) Allows the person to possess a concealed handgun on the developed property of the kindergarten through grade twelve (K-12) private school; or

(B) A kindergarten through grade twelve (K-12) private school or a prekindergarten private school that through its governing board or director has set forth the rules and circumstances under which the licensee may carry a concealed handgun into a building or event of the kindergarten through grade twelve (K-12) private school or the prekindergarten private school; or

(12) (A) The person has a license to carry a concealed handgun under § 5-73-301 et seq. and is carrying a concealed handgun in his or her motor vehicle or has left the concealed handgun in his or her locked and unattended motor vehicle in a publicly owned and maintained parking lot.

(B) (i) As used in this subdivision (e)(12), "parking lot" means a designated area or structure or part of a structure intended for the parking of motor vehicles or a designated drop-off zone for children at a school.

(ii) "Parking lot" does not include a parking lot owned, maintained, or otherwise controlled by the Division of Correction or Division of Community Correction.

History Acts 1989, No. 649, §§ 1-4; 1993, No. 1166, § 1; 1993, No. 1189, § 4; 1994 (2nd Ex. Sess.), No. 57, § 1; 1994 (2nd Ex. Sess.), No. 58, § 1; 1999, No. 1282, § 1; 2001, No. 592, § 1; 2005, No. 1994, § 476; 2013, No. 226, § 1; 2013, No. 746, § 1; 2013, No. 1390, § 1; 2015, No. 933, § 1; 2015, No. 1078, § 1; 2019, No. 472, § 1; 2019, No. 910, § 679.

§5-73-120. Carrying a weapon.

(a) A person commits the offense of carrying a weapon if he or she possesses a handgun, knife, or club on or about his or her person, in a vehicle occupied by him or her, or otherwise readily available for use with a purpose to attempt to unlawfully employ the handgun, knife, or club as a weapon against a person.

(b) As used in this section:

(1) "Club" means any instrument that is specially designed, made, or adapted for the purpose of inflicting serious physical injury or death by striking, including a blackjack, billie, and sap;

(2) "Handgun" means any firearm with a barrel length of less than twelve inches (12") that is designed, made, or adapted to be fired with one (1) hand;

(3) "Journey" means travel beyond the county in which a person lives; and

(4) "Knife" means any bladed hand instrument three inches (3") or longer that is capable of inflicting serious physical injury or death by cutting or stabbing, including a dirk, a sword or spear in a cane, a razor, an ice pick, a throwing star, a switchblade, and a butterfly knife.

(c) It is permissible to carry a weapon under this section if at the time of the act of carrying the weapon:

(1) The person is in his or her own dwelling or place of business or on property in which he or she has a possessory or proprietary interest;

(2) The person is a law enforcement officer, correctional officer, or member of the armed forces acting in the course and scope of his or her official duties;

(3) The person is assisting a law enforcement officer, correctional officer, or member of the armed forces acting in the course and scope of his or her official duties pursuant to the direction or request of the law enforcement officer, correctional officer, or member of the armed forces;

(4) The person is carrying a weapon when upon a journey, unless the journey is through a commercial airport when presenting at the security checkpoint in the airport or is in the person's checked baggage and is not a lawfully declared weapon;

(5) The person is a registered commissioned security guard acting in the course and scope of his or her duties;

(6) The person is hunting game with a handgun that may be hunted with a handgun under rules and regulations of the Arkansas State Game and Fish Commission or is en route to or from a hunting area for the purpose of hunting game with a handgun;

(7) (A) The person is a certified law enforcement officer, either on-duty or off-duty.

(B) If the person is an off-duty law enforcement officer, he or she may be required by a public school or publicly supported institution of higher education to be in physical possession of a valid identification identifying the person as a law enforcement officer;

(8) The person is in possession of a concealed handgun and has a valid license to carry a concealed handgun under § 5-73-301 et seq., or recognized under § 5-73-321 and is not in a prohibited place as defined by § 5-73-306;

(9) The person is a prosecuting attorney or deputy prosecuting attorney carrying a firearm under § 16-21-147; or

(10) The person is in possession of a handgun and is a retired law enforcement officer with a valid concealed carry authorization issued under federal or state law.

(d) Carrying a weapon is a Class A misdemeanor.

History Acts 1975, No. 696, § 1; 1981, No. 813, § 1; A.S.A. 1947, § 41-3151; Acts 1987, No. 266, § 1; 1987, No. 556, § 1; 1987, No. 734, § 1; 1995, No. 832, § 1; 2003, No. 1267, § 2; 2005, No. 1994, § 293; 2013; No. 539, § 2; 2013, No. 746, § 2; 2015, No. 1155, § 14; 2019, No. 472, § 2.

§5-73-121. [Repealed.]

§5-73-122. Carrying a firearm in publicly owned buildings or facilities.

(a) (1) Except as provided in § 5-73-322, § 5-73-306(5), § 16-21-147, and this section, it is unlawful for a person other than a law enforcement officer, either on-duty or off-duty, a security guard in the employ of the state or an agency of the state or any city or county, or any state or federal military personnel, to knowingly carry or possess a loaded firearm or other deadly weapon in any publicly owned building or facility or on the State Capitol grounds.

(2) It is unlawful for any person other than a law enforcement officer, either on-duty or off-duty, a security guard in the employ of the state or an agency of the state or any city or county, or any state or federal military personnel, to knowingly carry or possess a firearm, whether loaded or unloaded, in the State Capitol Building or the Arkansas Justice Building in Little Rock.

(3) However, this subsection does not apply to a person carrying or possessing a firearm or other deadly weapon in a publicly owned building or facility or on the State Capitol grounds:

(A) For the purpose of participating in a shooting match or target practice under the auspices of the agency responsible for the publicly owned building or facility or State Capitol grounds;

(B) If necessary to participate in a trade show, exhibit, or educational course conducted in the publicly owned building or facility or on the State Capitol grounds;

(C) (i) If the person has a license to carry a concealed handgun under § 5-73-301 et seq. and is carrying a concealed handgun in his or her motor vehicle or has left the concealed handgun in his or her locked and unattended motor vehicle in a publicly owned and maintained parking lot.

(ii) (a) As used in this subdivision (a)(3)(C), "parking lot" means a designated area or structure or part of a structure intended for the parking of motor vehicles or a designated drop-off zone for children at school.

(b) "Parking lot" does not include a parking lot owned, maintained, or otherwise controlled by:

(1) The Division of Correction;

(2) The Division of Community Correction; or

(3) A residential treatment facility owned or operated by the Division of Youth Services of the Department of Human Services;

(D) If the person has completed the required training and received a concealed carry endorsement under § 5-73-322(g) and the place is not:

(i) A courtroom or the location of an administrative hearing conducted by a state agency, except as permitted by § 5-73-306(5) or § 5-73-306(6);

(ii) A public school kindergarten through grade twelve (K-12), a public prekindergarten, or a public daycare facility, except as permitted under subdivision (a)(3)(C) of this section;

(iii) A facility operated by the Division of Correction or the Division of Community Correction; or

(iv) A posted firearm-sensitive area, as approved by the Department of Arkansas State Police under § 5-73-325, located at:

(a) The Arkansas State Hospital;

(b) The University of Arkansas for Medical Sciences; or

(c) A collegiate athletic event; or

(E) If the person has a license to carry a concealed handgun under § 5-73-301 et seq., is a justice of the Supreme Court or a judge on the Court of Appeals, and is carrying a concealed handgun in the Arkansas Justice Building.

(4) As used in this section, "facility" means a municipally owned or maintained park, football field, baseball field, soccer field, or another similar municipally owned or maintained recreational structure or property.

(b) However, a law enforcement officer, either on-duty or off-duty, officer of the court, bailiff, or other person authorized by the court is permitted to possess a handgun in the courtroom of any court or a courthouse of this state.

(c) A person violating this section upon conviction is guilty of a Class C misdemeanor.

(d) An off-duty law enforcement officer carrying a firearm in a publicly owned building or facility may be required to be in physical possession of a valid identification identifying the person as a law enforcement officer.

(e) An off-duty law enforcement officer may not carry a firearm into a courtroom if the off-duty law enforcement officer is a party to or a witness in a civil or criminal matter unless the law provides otherwise.

History Acts 1977, No. 549, §§ 1, 2; A.S.A. 1947, §§ 41-3113, 41-3114; Acts 1991, No. 1044, § 1; 1995, No. 1223, § 1; 1997, No. 910, § 1; 2013, No. 226, § 2; 2015, No. 1078, § 2; 2015, No. 1259, § 1; 2017, No. 562, § 1; 2017, No. 859, § 2; 2017, No. 1087, § 1; 2019, No. 472, §§ 3-5; 2019, No .910, §§ 680, 681; 2019, No. 431, § 1;.

§5-73-123. [Repealed.]

§5-73-124. Tear gas -- Pepper spray.

(a) (1) Except as otherwise provided in this section, any person who knowingly carries or has in his or her possession any tear gas or pepper spray in any form, or any person who knowingly carries or has in his or her possession any gun, bomb, grenade, cartridge, or other weapon designed for the discharge of tear gas or pepper spray, upon conviction is guilty of a Class A misdemeanor.

(2) (A) It is lawful for a person to possess or carry, and use, a container of tear gas or pepper spray to be used for self-defense purposes only.

(B) However, the capacity of the container shall not exceed one hundred fifty cubic centimeters (150 cc).

(b) The provisions of this section do not apply to any:

(1) Law enforcement officer while engaged in the discharge of his or her official duties; or

(2) Banking institution desiring to have possession of tear gas or pepper spray in any form for the purpose of securing funds in its custody from theft or robbery.

History Acts 1949, No. 338, §§ 1-3; 1977, No. 329, §§ 1, 2; A.S.A. 1947, §§ 41-3168 -- 41-3170; Acts 1993, No. 674, § 1; 1995, No. 1201, § 1; 2011, No. 1168, § 2; 2013, No. 1125, §§ 18, 19.

§5-73-125. Interstate sale and purchase of shotguns, rifles, and ammunition.

(a) The sale of shotguns and rifles and ammunition in this state to residents of other states is authorized under regulations issued by the United States Attorney General under the Gun Control Act of 1968, 18 U.S.C. § 921 et seq., as in effect on January 1, 2009.

(b) A resident of this state may purchase a rifle, shotgun, or ammunition in another state as expressly authorized under the regulations issued under the Gun Control Act of 1968, 18 U.S.C. § 921 et seq., as in effect on January 1, 2009.

History Acts 1969, No. 159, §§ 1, 2; A.S.A. 1947, §§ 41-3174, 41-3175; Acts 2009, No. 487, § 1.

§5-73-126. Booby traps.

(a) It is unlawful for any person to install or maintain a booby trap upon his or her own property or any other person's property.

(b) As used in this section, "booby trap" means a device designed to cause death or serious physical injury to a person.

(c) Any person who pleads guilty or nolo contendere or who is found guilty of violating this section is guilty of a Class D felony.

History Acts 1985, No. 243, §§ 1, 2; 1985, No. 399, §§ 1, 2; A.S.A. 1947, §§ 41-1660, 41-1661.

§5-73-127. Possession of loaded center-fire weapons in certain areas.

(a) It is unlawful to possess a loaded center-fire weapon, other than a shotgun and other than in a residence or business of the owner, in the following areas:

  (1) Baxter County:

   (A) That part bounded on the south by Highway 178, on the west and north by Bull Shoals Lake, and on the east by the Central Electric Power Corporation transmission line from Howard Creek to Highway 178;

   (B) That part of Bidwell Point lying south of the east-west road which crosses Highway 101 at the Presbyterian Church;

   (C) That part of Bidwell Point lying west of Bennett's Bayou and north of the east-west road which crosses Highway 101 at the Presbyterian Church;

   (D) That part of Baxter County between:

   (i) County Road 139 and Lake Norfork to the north and west;

   (ii) County Road 151 and Lake Norfork to the north, west, and south in the Diamond Bay area;

   (iii) The Bluff Road and Lake Norfork to the west;

   (iv) John Lewis Road (Timber Lake Manor) and Lake Norfork to the west and south;

   (v) The south end of County Road 91 south of its intersection with John Lewis Road and Lake Norfork to the south and east; and

   (vi) County Road 150 from its intersection with County Road 93 south and Lake Norfork to the south and east but not east of County Road 93;

  (2) Benton County:

   (A) That part of the Hobbs Estate north of State Highway 12, west of Rambo Road, and south and east of Van Hollow Creek and the Van Hollow Creek arm of Beaver Lake;

   (B) All of Bella Vista Village; and

(C) That part bounded on the north by Beaver Lake, on the east by Beaver Lake, on the south by the Hobbs State Management Area boundary from the intersection of State Highway 12 eastward along the boundary to its intersection with the Van Hollow Creek arm of Beaver Lake;

(3) Benton and Carroll Counties: That part bounded on the north by Highway 62, on the east by Highway 187 and Henry Hollow Creek, and the south and west by Beaver Lake and the road from Beaver Dam north to Highway 62;

(4) Conway County: That part lying above the rimrock of Petit Jean Mountain;

(5) Garland County: All of Hot Springs Village and Diamondhead;

(6) Marion County:

(A) That part known as Bull Shoals Peninsula, bounded on the east and north by White River and Lake Bull Shoals, on the west by the Jimmie Creek arm of Lake Bull Shoals, and on the south by the municipal boundaries of the City of Bull Shoals;

(B) That part of Marion County bounded on the north, west, and south by Bull Shoals Lake and on the east by County Roads 355 and 322 from their intersections with State Highway 202 to the points where they respectively dead-end at arms of Bull Shoals Lake;

(C) The Yocum Bend Peninsula of Bull Shoals Lake bounded on the north and east by Bull Shoals Lake, on the west by Pine Mountain and Bull Shoals Lake, and on the south by County Road 30; and

(D) Those lands situated in Marion County known as the Frost Point Peninsula, not inundated by the waters of Bull Shoals Lake, being more particularly described as follows:

(i) Section Six, Township Twenty North, Range Fifteen West, (Sec. 6 -- T.20 N. -- R.15 W.), lying south of the White River channel;

(ii) Section One, Township Twenty North, Range Sixteen West, (Sec. 1 -- T.20 N. -- R.16 W.); and

(iii) East Half of Section Two, Township Twenty North, Range Sixteen West, (E 1/2 Sec. 2 -- T.20 N. -- R.16 W.); North Half of the Northeast Quarter of Section Eleven, Township Twenty North, Range Sixteen West (N 1/2 -- NE 1/4 Sec. 11 -- T.20 N. -- R.16 W.); and

(7) A platted subdivision located in an unincorporated area.

(b) Nothing contained in this section shall be construed to limit or restrict or to make unlawful the discharge of a firearm in defense of a person or property within the areas described in this section.

(c) A person who is found guilty or who pleads guilty or nolo contendere to violating this section is guilty of a violation and shall be fined no less than twenty-five dollars ($25.00) nor more than five hundred dollars ($500).

(d) This section does not apply to a:

(1) Law enforcement officer in the performance of his or her duties;

(2) Discharge of a center-fire weapon at a firing range maintained for the discharging of a center-fire weapon; or

(3) Person possessing a valid concealed handgun license under § 5-73-301 et seq.

History Acts 1985, No. 515, §§ 1-3; 1987, No. 829, § 1; 1989, No. 63, § 1; 1991, No. 148, § 1; 1991, No. 731, § 1; 1993, No. 1099, § 1; 2007, No. 52, § 1; 2009, No. 748, § 40.

§5-73-128. Offenses upon property of public schools.

(a) (1) The court shall prepare and transmit to the Department of Finance and Administration an order of denial of driving privileges for a person within twenty-four (24) hours after the plea or finding, if a person who is less than nineteen (19) years of age at the time of the commission of the offense:

(A) Pleads guilty or nolo contendere to any criminal offense under § 5-73-101 et seq. or the Uniform Machine Gun Act, § 5-73-201 et seq., and the plea is accepted by the court, or is found guilty of any criminal offense under § 5-73-101 et seq. or the Uniform Machine Gun Act, § 5-73-201 et seq., if the state proves that the offense was committed upon the property of a public school or in or upon any school bus; or

(B) Is found by a juvenile division of circuit court to have committed an offense described in subdivision (a)(1)(A) of this section.

(2) In a case of extreme and unusual hardship, the order may provide for the issuance of a restricted driving permit to allow driving to and from a place of employment or driving to and from school.

(b) Upon receipt of an order of denial of driving privileges under this section, the department shall suspend the motor vehicle operator's license of the person for not less than twelve (12) months nor more than thirty-six (36) months.

(c) A penalty prescribed in this section is in addition to any other penalty prescribed by law for an offense covered by this section.

History Acts 1993, No. 264 §§ 1-3; 1993, No. 781, §§ 1-3.

§5-73-129. Furnishing a handgun or a prohibited weapon to a felon.

(a) A person commits the offense of furnishing a handgun to a felon if he or she sells, barters, leases, gives, rents, or otherwise furnishes a handgun to a person who he or she knows has been found guilty of or pleaded guilty or nolo contendere to a felony.

(b) A person commits the offense of furnishing a prohibited weapon to a felon if he or she sells, barters, leases, gives, rents, or otherwise furnishes

(1) A bomb;

(2) Metal knuckles;

(3) A defaced firearm, as described in § 5-73-107; or

(4) Other implement for the infliction of serious physical injury or death that serves no lawful purpose, to a person he or she knows has been found guilty of or who has pleaded guilty or nolo contendere to a felony.

(c) Furnishing a handgun or a prohibited weapon to a felon is a Class B felony.

History Acts 1994 (2nd Ex. Sess.), No. 41, § 1; 1994 (2nd Ex. Sess.), No. 42, § 1; 2019, No. 495, § 3; 2019, No. 1051, § 3.

§5-73-130. Seizure and forfeiture of firearm -- Seizure and forfeiture of motor vehicle -- Disposition of property seized.

(a) If a person under eighteen (18) years of age is unlawfully in possession of a firearm, the firearm shall be seized and, after an adjudication of delinquency or a conviction, is subject to forfeiture.

(b) If a felon or a person under eighteen (18) years of age is unlawfully in possession of a firearm in a motor vehicle, the motor vehicle is subject to seizure and, after an adjudication of delinquency or a conviction, subject to forfeiture.

(c) As used in this section, "unlawfully in possession of a firearm" does not include any act of possession of a firearm that is prohibited only by:

(1) Section 5-73-127, unlawful to possess loaded center-fire weapons in certain areas; or

(2) A regulation or rule of the Arkansas State Game and Fish Commission.

(d) The procedures for forfeiture and disposition of the seized property are as follows:

(1) The prosecuting attorney of the judicial district within whose jurisdiction the property is seized that is sought to be forfeited shall promptly proceed against the property by filing in the circuit court a petition for an order to show cause why the circuit court should not order forfeiture of the property; and

(2) The petition shall be verified and shall set forth:

(A) A statement that the action is brought pursuant to this section;

(B) The law enforcement agency bringing the action;

(C) A description of the property sought to be forfeited;

(D) A statement that on or about a date certain there was an adjudication of delinquency or a conviction and a finding that the property seized is subject to forfeiture;

(E) A statement detailing the facts in support of subdivision (d)(1) of this section; and

(F) A list of all persons known to the law enforcement agency, after diligent search and inquiry, who may claim an ownership interest in the property by title or registration or by virtue of a lien allegedly perfected in the manner prescribed by law.

(e) (1) Upon receipt of a petition complying with the requirements of subdivision (d)(1) of this section, the circuit court judge having jurisdiction shall issue an order to show cause setting forth a statement that this subchapter is the controlling law.

(2) In addition, the order shall set a date at least forty-one (41) days from the date of first publication of the order pursuant to subsection (f) of this section for all persons claiming an interest in the property to file such pleadings as they desire as to why the circuit court should not order the forfeiture of the property for use, sale, or other disposition by the law enforcement agency seeking forfeiture of the property.

(3) The circuit court shall further order that any person who does not appear on that date is deemed to have defaulted and waived any claim to the subject property.

(f) (1) The prosecuting attorney shall give notice of the forfeiture proceedings by:

(A) Causing a copy of the order to show cause to be published two (2) times each week for two (2) consecutive weeks in a newspaper having general circulation in the county where the property is located with the last publication being not less than five (5) days before the show cause hearing; and

(B) Sending a copy of the petition and order to show cause by certified mail, return receipt requested, to each person having ownership of or a security interest in the property or in the manner provided in Rule 4 of the Arkansas Rules of Civil Procedure if:

(i) The property is of a type for which title or registration is required by law;

(ii) The owner of the property is known in fact to the law enforcement agency at the time of seizure; or

(iii) The property is subject to a security interest perfected in accordance with the Uniform Commercial Code, § 4-1-101 et seq.

(2) The law enforcement agency is only obligated to make diligent search and inquiry as to the owner of the property, and if, after diligent search and inquiry, the law enforcement agency is unable to ascertain the owner, the requirement of actual notice by mail with respect to a person having a perfected security interest in the property is not applicable.

(g) At the hearing on the matter, the petitioner has the burden to establish that the property is subject to forfeiture by a preponderance of the evidence.

(h) In determining whether or not a motor vehicle should be ordered forfeited, the circuit court may take into consideration the following factors:

(1) Any prior criminal conviction or delinquency adjudication of the felon or juvenile;

(2) Whether or not the firearm was used in connection with any other criminal act;

(3) Whether or not the motor vehicle was used in connection with any other criminal act;

(4) Whether or not the juvenile or felon was the lawful owner of the motor vehicle in question;

(5) If the juvenile or felon is not the lawful owner of the motor vehicle in question, whether or not the lawful owner knew of the unlawful act being committed that gives rise to the forfeiture penalty; and

(6) Any other factor the circuit court deems relevant.

(i) The final order of forfeiture by the circuit court shall perfect in the law enforcement agency right, title, and interest in and to the property and shall relate back to the date of the seizure.

(j) Physical seizure of property is not necessary in order to allege in a petition under this section that the property is forfeitable.

(k) Upon filing the petition, the prosecuting attorney for the judicial district may also seek a protective order to prevent the transfer, encumbrance, or other disposal of any property named in the petition.

(l) The law enforcement agency to which a motor vehicle is forfeited shall either:

(1) Sell the motor vehicle in accordance with subsection (m) of this section; or

(2) If the motor vehicle is not subject to a lien that has been preserved by the circuit court, retain the motor vehicle for official use.

(m) (1) If a law enforcement agency desires to sell a forfeited motor vehicle, the law enforcement agency shall first cause notice of the sale to be made by publication at least two (2) times a week for two (2) consecutive weeks in a newspaper having general circulation in the county and by sending a copy of the notice of the sale by certified mail, return receipt requested, to each person having ownership of or a security interest in the property or in the manner provided in Rule 4 of the Arkansas Rules of Civil Procedure if:

(A) The property is of a type for which title or registration is required by law;

(B) The owner of the property is known in fact to the law enforcement agency at the time of seizure; or

(C) The property is subject to a security interest perfected in accordance with the Uniform Commercial Code, § 4-1-101 et seq.

(2) The notice of the sale shall include the time, place, and conditions of the sale and a description of the property to be sold.

(3) The property shall then be disposed of at public auction to the highest bidder for cash without appraisal.

(n) The proceeds of any sale and any moneys forfeited shall be applied to the payment of:

(1) The balance due on any lien preserved by the circuit court in the forfeiture proceedings;

(2) The cost incurred by the seizing law enforcement agency in connection with the storage, maintenance, security, and forfeiture of the property;

(3) The costs incurred by the prosecuting attorney or attorney for the law enforcement agency, approved by the prosecuting attorney, to which the property is forfeited; and

(4) Costs incurred by the circuit court.

(o) The remaining proceeds or moneys shall be deposited into a special county fund to be titled the "Juvenile Crime Prevention Fund", and the moneys in the fund shall be used solely for making grants to community-based nonprofit organizations that work with juvenile crime prevention and rehabilitation.

(p) (1) The law enforcement agency to which a firearm is forfeited may trade the firearm to a federally licensed firearms dealer for credit toward future purchases by the law enforcement agency.

(2) If the firearm is unable to be traded to a federally licensed firearms dealer, the law enforcement agency may dispose of the firearm as the law enforcement agency deems appropriate.

History Acts 1994 (2nd Ex. Sess.), No. 55, § 1; 1994 (2nd Ex. Sess.), No. 56, § 1; 2005, No. 1994, § 260; 2007, No. 827, § 96; 2019, No. 315, § 171, 2019, No. 630, §§ 1, 2.

§5-73-131. Possession or use of weapons by incarcerated persons.

(a) A person commits the offense of possession or use of weapons by incarcerated persons if, without approval of custodial authority he or she uses, possesses, makes, repairs, sells, or otherwise deals in any weapon, including, but not limited to, any bomb, firearm, knife, or other implement for the infliction of serious physical injury or death and that serves no common lawful

purpose, while incarcerated in the Division of Correction, the Division of Community Correction, or a county or municipal jail or detention facility.
(b) Possession or use of weapons by incarcerated persons is a Class D felony.
(c) This section is not applicable to possession of a weapon by an incarcerated person before he or she completes the standard booking and search procedures in a jail facility after arrest.
History Acts 1995, No. 443, § 1; 1995, No. 453, § 1; 2019, No. 910, § 682

§5-73-132. Sale, rental, or transfer of firearm to person prohibited from possessing firearms.

(a) A person shall not sell, rent, or transfer a firearm to any person who he or she knows is prohibited by state or federal law from possessing the firearm.
(b) (1) Violation of this section is a Class A misdemeanor, unless the firearm is:
    (A) A handgun;
    (B) An explosive or incendiary device, as defined in § 5-71-301;
    (C) A defaced firearm, as described in § 5-73-107; or
    (D) Other implement for the infliction of serious physical injury or death that serves no lawful purpose.
  (2) If the firearm is listed in subdivision (b)(1) of this section, a violation of this section is a Class B felony.
History Acts 1999, No. 1558, § 3; 2019, No. 495, § 4; 2019, No. 1051, § 4.

§5-73-133. Possession of a taser stun gun.

(a) As used in this section, "taser stun gun" means any device that:
  (1) Is powered by an electrical charging unit such as a battery; and
  (2) Either:
    (A) Emits an electrical charge in excess of twenty thousand (20,000) volts; or
    (B) Is otherwise capable of incapacitating a person by an electrical charge.
(b) (1) No person who is eighteen (18) years of age or under may purchase or possess a taser stun gun.
  (2) No person shall sell, barter, lease, give, rent, or otherwise furnish a taser stun gun to a person who is eighteen (18) years of age or under.
(c) Any law enforcement officer using a taser stun gun shall be properly trained in the use of the taser stun gun and informed of any danger or risk of serious harm and injury that may be caused by the use of the taser stun gun on a person.
(d) (1) A person who violates subdivision (b)(1) of this section is deemed guilty of an unclassified misdemeanor punishable by a fine of not less than five hundred dollars ($500) nor more than one thousand dollars ($1,000).
  (2) A person who violates subdivision (b)(2) of this section is deemed guilty of a Class B felony.
History Acts 2005, No. 2153, § 1.

STATUTE	LOCATION	EXCEPTION(S)
A.C.A. § 5-73-119(b)(1)	**(A)** Upon the developed property of a public or private school, kindergarten through grade twelve (K-12); **(B)** In or upon any school bus; or **(C)** At a designated bus stop as identified on the route list published by a school district each year.	**(e)(1)** The person is in his or her own dwelling or place of business or on property in which he or she has a possessory or proprietary interest, except upon the property of a public or private institution of higher learning; **(e)(2)** The person is a law enforcement officer, correctional officer, or member of the armed forces acting in the course and scope of his or her official duties; **(e)(3)** The person is assisting a law enforcement officer, correctional officer, or member of the armed forces acting in the course and scope of his or her official duties pursuant to the direction or request of the law enforcement officer, correctional officer, or member of the armed forces; **(e)(4)** The person is a registered commissioned security guard acting in the course and scope of his or her duties; **(e)(5)** The person is hunting game with a handgun or firearm that may be hunted with a handgun or firearm under the rules and regulations of the Arkansas State Game and Fish Commission or is en route to or from a hunting area for the purpose of hunting game with a handgun or firearm; **(e)(6)** The person is a certified law enforcement officer; **(e)(7)** The person is on a journey beyond the county in which the person lives, unless the person is eighteen (18) years of age or less; **(e)(8)** The person is participating in a certified hunting safety course sponsored by the commission or a firearm safety course recognized and approved by the commission or by a state or national nonprofit organization qualified and experienced in firearm safety; **(e)(9)** The person is participating in a school-approved educational course or sporting activity involving the use of firearms; **(e)(10)** The person is a minor engaged in lawful marksmanship competition or practice or other lawful recreational shooting under the supervision of his or her parent, legal guardian, or other person twenty-one (21) years of age or

		older standing in loco parentis or is traveling to or from a lawful marksmanship competition or practice or other lawful recreational shooting with an unloaded handgun or firearm accompanied by his or her parent, legal guardian, or other person twenty-one (21) years of age or older standing in loco parentis;
		(e)(11) The person has a license to carry a concealed handgun under A.C.A. § 5-73-301 et seq. and is carrying a concealed handgun on the developed property of:
		(A) A kindergarten through grade twelve (K-12) private school operated by a church or other place of worship that:
		(i) Is located on the developed property of the kindergarten through grade twelve (K-12) private school;
		(ii) Allows the person to carry a concealed handgun into the church or other place of worship under A.C.A. § 5-73-306; and
		(iii) Allows the person to possess a concealed handgun on the developed property of the kindergarten through grade twelve (K-12) private school; or
		(B) A kindergarten through grade twelve (K-12) private school or prekindergarten private school that through its governing board or director has set forth the rules and circumstances under which the licensee may carry a concealed handgun into a building or event of the kindergarten through grade twelve (K-12) private school or the prekindergarten private school; or
		(e)(12)(A) The person has a license to carry a concealed handgun under A.C.A. § 5-73-301 et seq. and is carrying a concealed handgun in his or her motor vehicle or has left the concealed handgun in his or her locked and unattended motor vehicle in a publicly owned and maintained parking lot.
		(B)(i) As used in this subdivision (e)(12), "parking lot" means a designated area or structure or part of a structure intended for the parking of motor vehicles or a designated drop-off zone for children at a school.
		(ii) "Parking lot" does not include a

		parking lot owned, maintained, or otherwise controlled by the Department of Correction or Department of Community Correction.
A.C.A. § 5-73-119(c)(1)	Upon the property of any private institution of higher education or a publicly supported institution of higher education in this state on or about his or her person, in a vehicle occupied by him or her, or otherwise readily available for use with a purpose to employ the handgun as a weapon against a person.	**(e)(1)** The person is in his or her own dwelling or place of business or on property in which he or she has a possessory or proprietary interest, except upon the property of a public or private institution of higher learning; **(e)(2)** The person is a law enforcement officer, correctional officer, or member of the armed forces acting in the course and scope of his or her official duties; **(e)(3)** The person is assisting a law enforcement officer, correctional officer, or member of the armed forces acting in the course and scope of his or her official duties pursuant to the direction or request of the law enforcement officer, correctional officer, or member of the armed forces; **(e)(4)** The person is a registered commissioned security guard acting in the course and scope of his or her duties; **(e)(5)** The person is hunting game with a handgun or firearm that may be hunted with a handgun or firearm under the rules and regulations of the Arkansas State Game and Fish Commission or is en route to or from a hunting area for the purpose of hunting game with a handgun or firearm; **(e)(6)** The person is a certified law enforcement officer; **(e)(7)** The person is on a journey beyond the county in which the person lives, unless the person is eighteen (18) years of age or less; **(e)(8)** The person is participating in a certified hunting safety course sponsored by the commission or a firearm safety course recognized and approved by the commission or by a state or national nonprofit organization qualified and experienced in firearm safety; **(e)(9)** The person is participating in a school-approved educational course or sporting activity involving the use of firearms; **(e)(10)** The person is a minor engaged in lawful marksmanship competition or practice or other lawful recreational shooting under the

		supervision of his or her parent, legal guardian, or other person twenty-one (21) years of age or older standing in loco parentis or is traveling to or from a lawful marksmanship competition or practice or other lawful recreational shooting with an unloaded handgun or firearm accompanied by his or her parent, legal guardian, or other person twenty-one (21) years of age or older standing in loco parentis; **(e)(11)** The person has a license to carry a concealed handgun under A.C.A. § 5-73-301 et seq. and is carrying a concealed handgun on the developed property of: **(A)** A kindergarten through grade twelve (K-12) private school operated by a church or other place of worship that: **(i)** Is located on the developed property of the kindergarten through grade twelve (K-12) private school; **(ii)** Allows the person to carry a concealed handgun into the church or other place of worship under A.C.A. § 5-73-306; and **(iii)** Allows the person to possess a concealed handgun on the developed property of the kindergarten through grade twelve (K-12) private school; or **(B)** A kindergarten through grade twelve (K-12) private school or prekindergarten private school that through its governing board or director has set forth the rules and circumstances under which the licensee may carry a concealed handgun into a building or event of the kindergarten through grade twelve (K-12) private school or the prekindergarten private school; or **(e)(12)(A)** The person has a license to carry a concealed handgun under A.C.A. § 5-73-301 et seq. and is carrying a concealed handgun in his or her motor vehicle or has left the concealed handgun in his or her locked and unattended motor vehicle in a publicly owned and maintained parking lot. **(B)(i)** As used in this subdivision (e)(12), "parking lot" means a designated area or structure or part of a structure intended for the parking of motor vehicles or a designated drop-

		off zone for children at a school.
		(ii) "Parking lot" does not include a parking lot owned, maintained, or otherwise controlled by the Department of Correction or Department of Community Correction.
		A.C.A. § 5-73-322(b) A licensee who has completed the training required under A.C.A. § 5-73-322(g) may possess a concealed handgun in the buildings and on the grounds of a public university, public college, or community college, whether owned or leased by the public university, public college, or community college, unless otherwise prohibited by:
		(d) The storage of a handgun in a university or college-operated student dormitory or residence hall is prohibited under A.C.A. § 5-73-119(c).
		(e)(1) A licensee who may carry a concealed handgun in the buildings and on the grounds of a public university, public college, or community college under this section may not carry a concealed handgun into a location in which an official meeting lasting no more than nine (9) hours is being conducted in accordance with documented grievance and disciplinary procedures as established by the public university, public college, or community college if:
		(A) At least twenty-four (24) hours' notice is given to participants of the official meeting;
		(B) Notice is posted on the door of or each entryway into the location in which the official meeting is being conducted that possession of a concealed handgun by a licensee under this section is prohibited during the official meeting; and
		(C) The area of a building prohibited under this subdivision (e)(1) is no larger than necessary to complete the grievance or disciplinary meeting.
		A.C.A. § 5-73-306
		A.C.A. § 5-73-322(c)(1) A licensee may possess a concealed handgun in the buildings and on the grounds of a private university or private college unless otherwise prohibited by

		this section or A.C.A. § 5-73-306 if the private university or private college does not adopt a policy expressly disallowing the carrying of a concealed handgun in the buildings and on the grounds of the private university or private college.
A.C.A. § 5-73-122(a)(1)	Publicly owned building or facility or on State Capitol grounds.	• As provided in **A.C.A. § 5-73-322(h)(1)** – carrying a firearm in a publicly owned building or facility under A.C.A. § 5-73-122, if the firearm is a concealed handgun; **A.C.A. § 5-73-306(5)** – courthouses as allowed; and **A.C.A. § 16-21-147(b)(3)** – prosecuting attorneys and those deputy prosecuting attorneys designated by prosecuting attorneys. • Law enforcement officer or security guard in the employ of the state or an agency of the state, or any city or county, or any state or federal military personnel. **(a)(3)(A)** For the purpose of participating in a shooting match or target practice under the auspices of the agency responsible for the publicly owned building or facility or State Capitol grounds. **(B)** If necessary to participate in a trade show, exhibit, or educational course conducted in the publicly owned building or facility or on the State Capitol grounds. **(C)(i)** If the person has a license to carry a concealed weapon under A.C.A. § 5-73-301 et seq. and is carrying a concealed handgun in his or her motor vehicle or has left the concealed handgun in his or her locked and unattended motor vehicle in a publicly owned and maintained parking lot. **(ii)(a)** As used in this subdivision (a)(3)(C), "parking lot" means a designated area or structure or part of a structure intended for the parking of motor vehicles or a designated drop-off zone for children at school. **(b)** "Parking lot" does not include a parking lot owned, maintained, or otherwise controlled by the Department of Correction or the Department of Community Correction. **(D)** If the person has completed the required

		training and received a concealed carry endorsement under A.C.A. § 5-73-322(g) and the place is not: (i) A courtroom or the location of an administrative hearing conducted by a state agency, except as permitted by A.C.A. § 5-73-306(5) or A.C.A. § 5-73-306(6); (ii) A public school kindergarten through grade twelve (K-12), a public prekindergarten, or a public daycare facility, except as permitted under subdivision (a)(3)(C) of this section; (iii) A facility operated by the Department of Correction or the Department of Community Correction; or (iv) A posted firearm-sensitive area, as approved by the Department of Arkansas State Police under A.C.A. § 5-73-325, located at: (a) The Arkansas State Hospital; (b) The University of Arkansas for Medical Sciences; or (c) A collegiate athletic event. (E) If the person has a license to carry a concealed handgun under A.C.A. § 5-73-301 et seq., is a justice of the Supreme Court or a judge on the Court of Appeals, and is carrying a concealed handgun in the Arkansas Justice Building. (b) A law enforcement officer, officer of the court, bailiff, or any other person authorized by the court is permitted to possess a handgun in the courtroom of any court or a courthouse of this state.
A.C.A. § 5-73-122(a)(2)	State Capitol Building or the Arkansas Justice Building in Little Rock.	• Law enforcement officer or security guard in the employ of the state or an agency of the state, or any city or county, or any state or federal military personnel. **A.C.A. § 5-73-322(h)(1)** A licensee who completes a training course and obtains a concealed carry endorsement under subsection (g) of this section is exempted from the prohibitions on: (1) Carrying a firearm in a publicly owned building or facility under A.C.A. § 5-73-122, if the firearm is a concealed handgun.
A.C.A. § 5-73-306(1)	Any police station. sheriff's station, or	

	Department of Arkansas State Police station.	
A.C.A. § 5-73-306(2)	An Arkansas Highway Police Division of the Arkansas Department of Transportation facility.	

A.C.A. § 5-73-306(3)	**(A)** A building of the Arkansas Department of Transportation or onto grounds adjacent to a building of the Arkansas Department of Transportation.	**(B)** This section does not apply to:
		    (i) A rest area or weigh station of the Arkansas Department of Transportation; or
		    (ii) A publicly owned and maintained parking lot that is a publicly accessible parking lot if the licensee is carrying a concealed handgun in his or her motor vehicle or has left the concealed handgun in his or her locked and unattended motor vehicle in the publicly owned and maintained parking lot.

A.C.A. § 5-73-306(4)	Any part of a detention facility, prison, or jail, including without limitation a parking lot owned or maintained or otherwise controlled by the Department of Correction or Department of Community Correction.	

A.C.A. § 5-73-306(5)	Any courthouse, courthouse annex, or other building owned, leased, or regularly used by a county for conducting court proceedings or housing a county office.	Unless:
		(A) The licensee is:
		    (i) Employed by the county;
		    (ii) A countywide official;
		    (iii) A justice of the peace; or
		    (iv)(a) Employed by a governmental entity other than the county with an office or place of employment inside the courthouse, the courthouse annex, or other building owned, leased, or regularly used by the county for conducting court proceedings or housing a county officer.

		(b) A licensee is limited to carrying a concealed handgun under subdivision (5)(A)(iv)(a) of this section into the courthouse, courthouse annex, or other building owned, leased, or regularly used by the county for conducting court proceedings, or housing a county office where the office or place of employment of the governmental entity that employs him or her is located. **(B)** The licensee's principal place of employment is within the courthouse, the courthouse annex, or other building owned, leased, or regularly used by the county for conducting court proceedings or housing a county office; and **(C)** The quorum court by ordinance approves a plan that allows licensees permitted to carry under this subdivision (5) to carry a concealed handgun into the courthouse, courthouse annex, or other building owned, leased, or regularly used by a county for conducting court proceedings as set out by the local security and emergency preparedness plan.
A.C.A. § 5-73-306(6)	**(A)** Any courtroom.	**(B)** However, nothing in this subchapter precludes a judge from carrying a concealed weapon or determining who will carry a concealed weapon into his or her courtroom.
A.C.A. § 5-73-306(7)	Any meeting place of the governing body of any governmental unit.	**A.C.A. § 5-73-322(h)(i)(2)** – A licensee who completes a training course and obtains a concealed carry endorsement under subsection (g) of this section is exempted from the prohibition and restriction on carrying a concealed handgun in a prohibited place listed under A.C.A. § 5-73-306(7).
A.C.A. § 5-73-306(8)	Any meeting of the General Assembly or a committee of the General Assembly.	**A.C.A. § 5-73-322(h)(i)(2)** – A licensee who completes a training course and obtains a concealed carry endorsement under subsection (g) of this section is exempted from the prohibition and restriction on carrying a concealed handgun in a prohibited place listed under A.C.A. § 5-73-306(8).
A.C.A. § 5-73-306(9)	Any state office.	**A.C.A. § 5-73-322(h)(i)(2)** – A licensee who completes a training course and obtains a concealed carry endorsement under subsection (g) of this section is exempted from the prohibition and restriction on carrying a

		concealed handgun in a prohibited place listed under A.C.A. § 5-73-306(9).
A.C.A. § 5-73-306(10)	Any athletic event not related to firearms.	**A.C.A. § 5-73-322(h)(i)(2)** – A licensee who completes a training course and obtains a concealed carry endorsement under subsection (g) of this section is exempted from the prohibition and restriction on carrying a concealed handgun in a prohibited place listed under A.C.A. § 5-73-306(10).
A.C.A. § 5-73-306(11)	**(A)** A portion of an establishment, except a restaurant as defined in A.C.A. § 3-5-1202, licensed to dispense alcoholic beverages on the premises.	**A.C.A. § 5-73-322(h)(i)(2)** – A licensee who completes a training course and obtains a concealed carry endorsement under subsection (g) of this section is exempted from the prohibition and restriction on carrying a concealed handgun in a prohibited place listed under A.C.A. § 5-73-306(11). EXCEPT **A.C.A. § 5-73-306(11)(B)** A person with a concealed carry endorsement under A.C.A. § 5-73-322(g) and who is carrying a concealed handgun may not enter an establishment under this section if the establishment either places a written notice as permitted under subdivision (18) of this section or provides notice under subdivision (19) of this section prohibiting a person with a license to possess a concealed handgun at the physical location.
A.C.A. § 5-73-306(12)	**(A)** A portion of an establishment, except a restaurant as defined in A.C.A. § 3-5-1202, where beer or light wine is consumed on the premises.	**A.C.A. § 5-73-322(h)(i)(2)** – A licensee who completes a training course and obtains a concealed carry endorsement under subsection (g) of this section is exempted from the prohibition and restriction on carrying a concealed handgun in a prohibited place listed under A.C.A. § 5-73-306(12). EXCEPT **A.C.A. § 5-73-306(12)(B)** A person with a concealed carry endorsement under A.C.A. § 5-73-322(g) and who is carrying a concealed handgun may not enter an establishment under this section if the establishment either places a written notice as permitted under subdivision (18) of this section or provides notice under subdivision (19) of this section prohibiting a person with a license to possess a concealed handgun at the physical location.

A.C.A. § 5-73-306(13)	(A) A school, college, community college, or university campus building or event.	(B) However, subdivision (13)(A) does not apply to: (i) A kindergarten through grade twelve (K-12) private school operated by a church or other place of worship that: (a) Is located on the developed property of the kindergarten through grade twelve (K-12) private school; (b) Allows the licensee to carry a concealed handgun into the church or other place of worship under this section; and (c) Allows the licensee to possess a concealed handgun on the developed property of the kindergarten through grade twelve (K-12) private school under A.C.A. § 5-73-119(e). (ii) A kindergarten through grade twelve (K-12) private school or prekindergarten private school that through its governing board or director has set forth the rules and circumstances under which the licensee may carry a concealed handgun into a building or event of the kindergarten through grade twelve (K-12) private school or the prekindergarten private school; (iii) Participation in an authorized firearms-related activity; (iv) Carrying a concealed handgun as authorized under A.C.A. § 5-73-322; or (v) A publicly owned and maintained parking lot of a college, community college, or university if the licensee is carrying a concealed handgun in his or her motor vehicle or has left the concealed handgun in his or her locked and unattended motor vehicle.
A.C.A. § 5-73-306(14)	Inside the passenger terminal of any airport, except that no person is prohibited from carrying any legal firearm into the passenger terminal if the firearm is encased for shipment for purposes of	**A.C.A. § 5-73-322(h)(i)(2)** – A licensee who completes a training course and obtains a concealed carry endorsement under subsection (g) of this section is exempted from the prohibition and restriction on carrying a concealed handgun in a prohibited place listed under A.C.A. § 5-73-306(14).

	checking the firearm as baggage to be lawfully transported on any aircraft.	
A.C.A. § 5-73-306(15)	**(A)** Any church or other place of worship.	**(B)** However, this subchapter does not preclude a church or other place of worship from determining who may carry a concealed handgun into the church or other place of worship. **A.C.A. § 5-73-322(h)(i)(2)** – A licensee who completes a training course and obtains a concealed carry endorsement under subsection (g) of this section is exempted from the prohibition and restriction on carrying a concealed handgun in a prohibited place listed under A.C.A. § 5-73-306(15). EXCEPT **A.C.A. § 5-73-306(15)(C)** A person with a concealed carry endorsement under A.C.A. § 5-73-322(g) and who is carrying a concealed handgun may not enter an establishment under this section if the establishment either places a written notice as permitted under subdivision (18) of this section or provides notice under subdivision (19) of this section prohibiting a person with a license to possess a concealed handgun at the physical location.
A.C.A. § 5-73-306(16)	Any place where the carrying of a firearm is prohibited by federal law.	
A.C.A. § 5-73-306(17)	Any place where a parade or demonstration requiring a permit is being held, and the licensee is a participant in the parade or demonstration.	**A.C.A. § 5-73-322(h)(i)(2)** – A licensee who completes a training course and obtains a concealed carry endorsement under subsection (g) of this section is exempted from the prohibition and restriction on carrying a concealed handgun in a prohibited place listed under A.C.A. § 5-73-306(17).
A.C.A. § 5-73-306(18)	**(A)(i)** Any place at the discretion of the person or entity exercising control	**(B)** Subdivision (18)(A) of this section does not apply if the place is: **(i)** A public university, public college, or community college, as defined in A.C.A. § 5-

	over the physical location of the place by placing at each entrance to the place a written notice clearly readable at a distance of not less than ten feet (10') that "carrying a handgun is prohibited." **(i)(a)** If the place does not have a roadway entrance, there shall be a written notice placed anywhere upon the premises of the place. **(b)** In addition to the requirement of subdivision (18)(A)(ii)(a) of this section, there shall be at least one (1) written notice posted within every three (3) acres of a place with no roadway entrance. **(iii)** A written notice as described in subdivision (18)(A)(i) of this section is not required for a private home. **(iv)** Any licensee entering a private home shall notify the occupant that the licensee is carrying a concealed handgun.	73-322, and the licensee is carrying a concealed handgun as provided under A.C.A. § 5-73-322. **(ii)** A publicly owned and maintained parking lot if the licensee is carrying a concealed handgun in his or her motor vehicle or has left the concealed handgun in his or her locked and unattended motor vehicle; or **(iii)** A parking lot of a private employer and the licensee is carrying a concealed handgun as provided under A.C.A. § 5-73-326.
A.C.A. § 5-73-306(19)	**(A)(i)** A place	

	owned or operated by a private entity that prohibits the carrying of a concealed handgun that posts a written notice as described under subdivision (18)(A) of this section. **(ii)(a)** A place owned or operated by a private entity that chooses not to post a written notice as described under subdivision (18)(A) of this section may provide written or verbal notification to a licensee who is carrying a concealed handgun at the place owned or operated by a private entity that carrying of a concealed handgun is prohibited. **(b)** A licensee who receives written or verbal notification under subdivision (19)(A)(ii)(a) of this section is deemed to have violated this subdivision (19) if the licensee while carrying a concealed handgun either remains at or returns to the place owned or operated	

	by the private entity. **(B)** A place owned or operated by a private entity under this subdivision (19) includes without limitation: (i) A private university or private college; (ii) A church or other place of worship; (iii) An establishment, except a restaurant as defined in A.C.A. § 3-5-1202, licensed to dispense alcoholic beverages for consumption on the premises; and (iv) An establishment, except a restaurant as defined in A.C.A. § 3-5-1202, where beer or light wine is consumed on the premises.	
A.C.A. § 5-73-306(20)	A posted firearm-sensitive area, as approved by the Department of Arkansas State Police under A.C.A. § 5-73-325, located at: **(A)** The Arkansas State Hospital; **(B)** The University of Arkansas for Medical Sciences;	

	or **(C)** A collegiate athletic event.